ARISE

FROM BENEATH THE RUBBLE

CHARLES DIXON

Copyright © 2022 by Charles Dixon.

ISBN   Softcover   978-1-956998-08-5

All rights reserved. No part of this book may be reproduced or transmitted in any form or by any means, electronic or mechanical, including photocopying, recording, or by any information storage and retrieval system without express written permission from the author, except in the case of brief quotations embodied in critical reviews and certain other non-commercial uses permitted by copyright law.

To order additional copies of this book, contact:
Bookwhip
1-855-339-3589
https://www.bookwhip.com

Arise from beneath the Rubble

A Spirited Hundred-Year Journey of African American Men's and Families' Strength in Forging Ahead through Obstacles of Racism, Crime, Violence, War, and Poverty of the Past and Present

CONTENTS

Acknowledgments vii

Introduction ix

I   Long Red Clay Trail 1

II   Dark Dreary Days 16

III   Taking It to the Streets 27

IV   Don't Open the Door 42

V   Who's at the Door? The Vietnam War 49

VI   The Men's Movement 57

VII Three Hots and a Cot 68

VIII Jewels and the Crown 76

IX   Tools and Approaches to Empower Men, Families, and Communities 91

X   Community Alliances or Partnerships 110

Endnotes 119

ACKNOWLEDGMENTS

This book is a tribute to the legacy of wonderful individuals who deeply influenced and inspired my life. These individuals helped shape my purpose and destiny. They also laid the foundation of my growth and development, certainly for my greater good.

I humbly celebrate several men and women for their contributions to my life. I salute my parents; both of them contributed to whom I have become. First, my father was a conscientious man who loved his family and wanted the best for his children. Although having health challenges, he gave his best and wanted the best for his children and family. Even being separated from my mother, he stayed always near. We knew and acknowledged his presence he showed through his principles and family values.

Second, I salute my mother, who is and was greatly appreciated and valued for her steadfastness and labors of love. Having eight children was more than a challenge, but Ms. Emma Bell Dixon could and would handle any situation on any given day. In a sense, she was weather-proof; whatever storm came, she knew and believed a shelter was somewhere—not over the rainbow. Someway, somehow, all the children and others would get there safely. She was a remarkable and phenomenal woman who glimpsed heaven through her spiritual relationship with God. Her accomplishment of raising constructive, energetic, well-versed children by hook, crook, pelt, and brick was a true testament of love. As a child,

I never understood that the discipline hurt her more than it did the one receiving it. She used the method not found in textbooks called *applied psychology*; she applied her hand or any method used to resolve matters related to children's lack of discipline—sometimes called a *whippin'*—whenever needed.

And finally, I salute a spiritual giant whose name reverberates in the hearts of countless men and women across the world, the Reverend Dr. Arturo Skinner, who served as a catalyst in refining the Pentecostal movement in America. But personally, his love for my family was supreme. (Not being selfish, he loved other families as well.) He gave us a personal touch. He was the village leader, ensuring the health of families and communities. His love and support had no limitation. Although he was a man's man, he exhibited love. I contribute much of my life to the seed that he planted through his prayers, commitment, and vision toward a better humanity through his faith in God. My family, along with countless hosts of men, saluted him for his servanthood to God and his commitment to uplifting families and encouraging them to succeed.

INTRODUCTION

For a quarter century in my adult years, I have been fortunate to work as a community advocate for thousands of young men and families in an urban community such as Newark, New Jersey. I've sort of found it easy to advocate for families because in my own childhood, I had seven brothers and sisters, along with family friends, and relatives, and seemingly knowing the entire community. I lived in *brick city*, also known as the projects. My childhood helped set the tone for working with young men and families. As a child, I had a life filled with happy moments, even while we lived in poverty. I really didn't know of our impoverished status until years later, when I grew up, because I felt wealthy. The world's greatest men and women surrounded me, especially my brothers and sisters and other family members.

Years later, I discovered we had an incredible treasure; that was my family. Despite our challenges, we had unbreakable spirits that no one could defeat. We came from good stock—family values, community support, and spiritual values. We had neighbors who envied us because we were blessed. Our family represented thousands of other families that live in urban impoverished communities yet are rich in family, striving to improve. But as you grow up, the stories of the black community at some point become dismal and full of misfortune and doom, especially about black males and their families.

As I matured into adulthood, for as long as I can remember (nearly half a century), reports and the news alerted us of the crisis of black males in America. The reports were televised and featured in magazine and journal articles. They reported the high rates of incarceration, poor health conditions, high school dropouts, a lack of college education, teenage pregnancy, and so on among young men. These reports and articles prompted me to ask the question "Why are there such disparities among African Americans, especially the males?" These overwhelming statistics have bombarded us as a society, leaving viewer and reader with images of despair and hopelessness of this race.

These images made me inquisitive about why this despair existed among the African American race, unlike any other race. I became eager to know what transpired in America that seemed to have impacted blacks in such a negative manner. I wanted to understand the social conditions and circumstances that influenced African American men and their families. These reports of such crisis baffled me, because history illustrates to the world blacks have been known for our greatness in the development of early civilizations. We were inventors of sciences and medicine and agriculture, builders of cities and empires throughout the world and advanced arts and culture; the list of greatness resounds through the corridors of time for African American people. Therefore, I ventured back approximately one hundred years to view the past, only a small portion or a glimpse of American history, to better understand the present and to safeguard future generations against such social and moral deterioration and decay.

Working with young men in urban communities across the nation for more than two decades, I have experienced the lives of men and families miraculously restored and revitalized. I have experienced young men obtaining careers, jobs, guidance, and direction for their lives and becoming leaders of both their families and communities. Thousands of men and families have become renewed and empowered to live healthy and productive lives. The young have arisen from beneath the social stigma and rubble of despair.

This autobiography entered my world so family members and relatives can view both our community's and the nation's impact on the development of men or fathers and families. In this book, I peer out the window of my soul; it reveals the pain, suffering, agony, and victory of black Americans. It's a journey of the trials and triumphs of family members, the community, and even America, one hundred years in the making. It will discuss the social ingredients in the development and shaping of black men in our America. It will illustrate women's significant roles in aiding and supporting men to achieve success. Ultimately, it reveals approaches and tools to fortify families, especially among our men.

> *"For I know the Plans I have for you…to prosper you, not to harm you, plans to give you a Future filled with hope ."*
>
> —*Jeremiah 29:11.*

LONG RED CLAY TRAIL

As a young boy, I remember hearing stories of my mother, Ms. Emma B. Dixon, when she was a little girl. My mother and father; my seven siblings, Bobby, Arzelia, Original, Margie, Edward, Jerry, and Carl; and I all had to take time to listen to her stories. Sometimes, in the kitchen or the living room or walking to the store or anywhere, my mother would tell us stories about growing up in the South. It was like an adventure through Wonderland. It gave us the opportunity to experience her world growing up in the South. Certainly, it was different from our experience growing up in the city, with fast cars, buses, trains, airplanes, mass transportation, television, and radio.

On June 12, 1925, my mother was born to Sula B. Woods. They lived in Fort Gaines in the peach state of Georgia. They lived at least four miles from any neighbor—deep in the woods, which people sometimes call the *sticks*—in a big brown wooden house that accommodated ten children and a mother and father. In front of the house was Old Red Clay Road that led into town toward neighbors' houses and school, and that led anyone into this rural farmland. This road seemed to run into eternity.

Emma Bell Woods Dixon as a little girl living in Fort Gaines, Georgia

There, my mother's family had a farm with chickens, pigs, mules, cows, a donkey, and lots of vegetation, such as peanuts, corn, peas, tomatoes, and even cotton. During the spring, the crops would grow. When the children weren't in school, they had to be the caretakers for the farm's crops. They had to get up at about 5:00 or 6:00 a.m. to work on the farm. At that time, children could start working at five or six years of age. They all had responsibilities, from the youngest to the oldest, whether that meant picking cotton, peas, or corn or milking the cow, placing a bucket beneath the cow and squeezing its nipples to get milk. Everybody had a job from sunup to sundown.

On those hot, steamy days, they always needed to get work done. If you worked in the field, you had many dangers to overcome, such as snakes lying on the ground alongside the crops or other wild animals roaming the farm, such as dogs, foxes, and other stray animals. It could be dangerous. Their father protected them from harm. He had a shotgun in case of any threatening situations. It hung up in the front room in case of intruders.

Fortunately, the children didn't have to work all year, only seasonally. The other seasons, like fall and spring, they attended school. Black children attended separate schools from white children. The South was segregated; it functioned under Jim Crow laws during that time. Some sections were for blacks and other sections for whites. My mother told us they would walk six to seven miles to school each day. They didn't have a car or any other mode of transportation to get to school, so they had a long journey on Long Red Clay Trail, there and back. Each day Monday to Friday, they attended school, carrying books or clothing needed for school.

Old Red Clay Road in Fort Gaines, Georgia,
which the children and family walked daily

As my mother and her siblings traveled to or from school, as black children, sometimes white children would tease them, say horrible things, and throw paper or other objects at them along Long Red Clay

Trail. Sometimes, the road seemed like an eternity. Kennon Grove Elementary School was joined to Kennon Grove Baptist Church, and family plots or grave sites were behind the church. Each day, school was held from 8:15 a.m. to 3:30 p.m. The school had only two classes: one for the lower grades and the other for the upper-class students. The entire school had approximately fifteen to twenty students.

The school day would begin with a prayer and the Pledge of Allegiance or a salute to the American flag. The student lessons were for reading, spelling, and math. The first part of the day consisted of students engaging in reading assignments. They had to participate in the learning process, completing homework and classroom reading lessons and responding to questions to understand the homework. It wasn't optional for the students to be active participants. Everyone had to participate in discussing a lesson. If the students disobeyed a teacher, there were consequences. The teachers were allowed to discipline the students by spanking or whipping them. Once in a while, they took a student outside and beat him or her with switches. The parents accepted this. Furthermore, if the parents heard of their son getting a whipping by the teacher, the parents would follow suit and whip the youngster at home.

After the morning classes, the children would go to lunch. They had hot meals cooked on the premises, as they had a cooking facility. They used a potbelly stove to cook pork 'n' beans and rice. They didn't have a large variety of food for lunch. When the students finished eating, they played outside in the field. They jumped rope and played other games. One game in particular was a sing-along game. The lyric to the song, "Old Red Clay Road–Greenfield Rocky Love," was as follows: "Can't you tell me who you love?" They repeated that three times. The song leader would go to the middle of the field near the schoolhouse. Then, he or she would call a person over to sit in the front, about ten feet away from the person in the middle of the field. They would repeat the song: "Can't you tell me who you love?" The song leader would then call the person's name. Then, they loved to sit by the school wall. The game would continue until almost all the children were selected. Well, if the children were not selected, they had to get the next game.

Then, they returned back to the classroom. The afternoon included math or spelling for the entire afternoon. As the school day ended, the students returned to Long Red Clay Trail, traveling six to seven miles back home. Years later, the students transferred to the Chattahoochee Grammar School in Fort Gaines, Georgia. But the school experienced a tornado, and it was destroyed. The students were then transferred to States High School in Georgia.

Each day was a journey for the children, whether going to school or working on the farm. Obviously, they didn't have lots of luxuries. Their parents were strict, so they were accounted for at all times. Mothers and fathers knew where their children were or were supposed to be. They always had accountability. Even if they had to work for the white man (whom they identified as *Mr. Charlie*), they would pick up the children early in the morning and take them back home at the end of the day. The children would get two dollars on from the farm owner. During that time, they earned a good income, especially at twelve years of age.

As the children became teenagers, the boys and girls began to mature and have social lives. They began to date; if a young lady was courting or was interested in a boy, he would come to the house, sit in the living room, and meet the family. One of the sons, my mother's brother, Uncle Frank, said sometimes, the date would work on the farm with the mate, I guess to see the way he or she would fair working in the field, doing chores. Perhaps the family observed if the relationship had long-term potential. However, if the date visiting the house stayed too close to nightfall, the father would walk through the living room. That meant the date had to leave. The worst thing in the world was for the father to tell the date to leave, because the date may not get welcomed back.

My uncle Frank stated boys weren't as likely to act promiscuously or have sex before marriage back then. If a young man ever got a young lady pregnant, he would more than likely marry her or leave town, because the young lady's father would go gunning for him. The girl's daddy would literally go to the young man's house with his shotgun. The young man would either prepare for a wedding on the spot or get ready for his own funeral. The father overprotected or safeguarded his family by any means necessary. The father made sure to maintain order in the house. He was the enforcer.

On the other hand, the mother made sure the house functioned properly. She made sure all the ducks lined up. That meant all the chores—cleaning, cooking, and clothes—were done and the meals were adequately prepared for the husband and children. Every day, they had dinner on the table. The wife prepared the meals, whether she had the chickens or some other animal killed. In this particular case, this was my grandmother.

My grandmother, Mrs. Sula B. Woods, was a most influential and fascinating person. She was the queen of mothers. She had ten children: Unis, Mary, Margie, Emma, James, Joe, Johnny, Bobby, Eli, and Frank. Sula Woods worked in a peanut factory, picked cotton, and went to town to sell vegetables, including corn, carrying them over her head in a basket. She was a sharecropper. She worked on what was really the white men's land; they were the caretakers of the land. They had to pay the owners half of whatever they received or made on the land. Mother Sula worked hard, and the children also worked from the age of seven or eight. They worked for the white man as well. Oftentimes, they worked from 6:00 a.m. to 6:00 p.m. Sometimes, they got paid sixty cents. The white farm owners would go to the house to pick up the kids and take them to work on their farm.

My mother, Emma Woods Dixon; my grandmother, Sula B. Woods; Aunt Unis; Uncle Bobby; and Uncle Eli

Grandmom was the CEO of the house, while her husband was like the president. My grandmother managed the house's daily operations, such as preparing dinner. She would cook everything from scratch; to make pancakes or biscuits, she would pour flour into a bowl, add their cow's milk and chickens' eggs, and stir up the batter and churn butter. They had a smokehouse that preserved pig and cow meat; they had meat for any occasion. They were self-sufficient. They didn't have modern facilities or appliances, like a refrigerator to preserve food or a bathroom for washing and other uses. They had to go into the woods' shade to go to the potty. The children and family had to be careful because sometimes snakes would hide in the shade.

When it came to washing clothes back then, Grandmom had to travel four to five miles to the spring on Old Red Clay Road. It made for an all-day, tedious task. She would carry the clothes for the ten children, herself, and her husband on her back and in her hands. Before washing the clothes, she first had to heat a huge pot of water. She would put logs and sticks under a pot of water. Then she would place the clothes in the pot with lye soap and churn the clothes with a stick. Afterward, she would take the clothes out, place them on a hard surface, and beat the clothes with a large wooden object to beat the stains out of them. Then, she would rinse them a second and third time. Finally, she would hang them on a clothesline to dry. This was an all-day event. She had to head to the spring early in the morning so the sun's heat could dry the clothes. She did this at least once a week.

Certainly, the weekend was mostly for chores, like Fridays. On Saturdays, the boys went with their father into town seven to eight miles down that Old Red Clay Road. They would take the buggy to town. All the boys would sit in the back of the buggy. They enjoyed two main activities. First, when they went into Fort Gaines, they bought candy downtown as a treat. They didn't have local stores, so once a week, they could really enjoy themselves, purchasing candy. The second activity they really valued was listening to the radio. Because they didn't have a television (which wasn't invented yet), the radio was their means of maintaining contact with the rest of the world. They would laugh and be amused by fights, like Joe Louis versus Max Schmeling, and stories on the radio.

Sons Eli Woods and Bobby Woods

Sundays meant family and friends all day long. That day, everybody went to church, Kennon Grove Baptist Church. Reverend Gaines was the pastor. Old Kennon Grove was the hot spot for everybody. The people in the community revered the church, as if God sat in the congregation. Sunday service was a community event. The service went from 9:30 a.m. to 5:00 p.m. Everybody had to go to church. Everyone had to press their clothes. Everyone had to look their best when going to church. The women and girls wore their big wide hats, and the men and boys wore their suits.

When they got to church, they had a good time singing, with hands clapping and feet stomping on the wooden floors. Reverend Gaines would give a soul-stirring message to the congregation. Every now and then, someone would start shouting or jumping up and down. They rejoiced about their faith or their hardships in life. After the message, they would have an opening prayer. The entire congregation would pray, each person, one by one. They had what they called the *mourners' bench* when they would have a special prayer for people who had serious needs or requests for God. One person would start praying, and simultaneously, the next person would pray as well. Then, the preacher would bring a message of hope for the members to have faith in God. It was call-and-response. They would travail in prayer for congregation members. After the service, dinner was served. Everyone who could cook would participate and provide their best meal. When dinner ended, the service began again. Sunday was known as *God's Day*. All day long, they had to honor it by being in the church.

Kennon Grove Baptist Church in Fort Gaines, Georgia

My mother told us stories of misfortune and heartache about that Long Red Clay Trail leading into town. At times, the family was overwhelmed. Sometimes, residing in the South wasn't always a pleasant experience, especially when it came to mistreating brothers and sisters. My mother remembered her grandpa singing a song called "There's a Leak in the Building," which went, "There's a leak in the building. I got to move to a better home. It's a-raining in this building, but I got to move." She told stories of the South that we found amusing and unthinkable. She had fond memories of her great-grandpa, Jim Mathis. She said when Jim sang that, people came from afar just to hear him.

It was said Jim Mathis was a former slave. His father was a white man. Mr. Mathis had several wives. He outlived all his wives. He had faced many adversities living in the South post-slavery. My mother told a story Grandpa told of white men who lived together. They kept their families in one house. But they also had another house where black women were housed. It was said the white men would rape the black women and have children by these women. They were housed originally for the purpose of working on the farm. Months after these acts, these women would have children. After these women delivered the babies, they would have to resume work, and they would leave the children in something like a trough, or pigpen, until the workday was over. The children would lie in the heat of the day, not nurtured or loved—forgotten.

Grandpa experienced many traumatic situations, even the death of his brother. He spoke to his granddaughter, my mother, one day about it. When his brother was in town, he had an argument with one of the white men in town. After the conflict, as his brother walked home, the white men came seeking to harm him. They found him on the way home and shot and killed him in cold blood. Black men weren't allowed to speak up for themselves. It was said white men wanted to "keep Niggers in their place."

Mr. and Ms. Jim Mathis in the early 1900s

Jim Mathis was a man of standards, even though he had five wives and numerous children. He maintained standards. When it came to having his children married, he wanted to make sure everything was in order. It was said Jim Mathis would not let a young man marry his daughter because he went to a club and came back drunk one night. Jim Mathis threatened to kill him if he came to the house drunk and messed with his daughter. During that time, the father was the boss. Whatever he said was law. Jim Mathis was important and highly respected.

Jim Mathis in the 1930s

It was said that Jeff Woods, a former slave, received a will, and a landowner gave one hundred acres of land to him. He married one of the daughters of Jim Mathis, Sula B. Woods. Then, over many years of toiling and working, Mother Sula purchased land and built a house for her family. She moved to the city. In order to support themselves, they became migrant workers. They traveled the entire coast, working for people on their farms, commuting from south to north, Florida to upstate New York.

> *The ultimate measure of a man is not where he stands in moments of comfort and convenience, but where he stands at times of challenge and controversy.*
>
> *—Dr. Martin Luther King Jr.*

Discussion Questions & Exercises

Vocabulary Words
Share Croppers
Post-Slavery
Tedious

Old Red Clay Road

My mother's family had a farm with chickens, pigs, mules, cows, a donkey, and lots of vegetation, such as peanuts, corn, peas, tomatoes, and even cotton. Living on the farm was tedious. During the spring, the crops would grow. When the children weren't in school, they had to be the caretakers for the farm's crops. The children had various responsibilities and chores each day. They had to get up at about 5:00 a.m. to work on the farm. Children could start working at five years of age. Each child had responsibilities, from the youngest to the oldest, whether that meant picking cotton, peas, corn or milking the cow. Everybody had a job from sunup to sundown.

1. What were some of your responsibilities growing up in your home?

_____

_____

_____

_____

_____

If you worked in the field, you had many dangers to overcome, such as snakes lying on the ground alongside the crops or other wild animals roaming the farm, such as dogs, foxes, and other stray animals. It could be dangerous. Their father used a shotgun to protect them from harm. It would hang in the front room in case of intruders.

2. What role did your father play in your life when growing up?

_____

_____

_____

_____

My grandmother managed the household's daily operations. She would cook everything from scratch; to make pancakes or biscuits, she would use the cow's milk and chickens' eggs, stir up the batter and churn butter. They had a smokehouse that preserved pig and cow meat; they had meat for any occasion.

3. What role did your grandmother play in your life when growing up?

4. How did you feel about your parents growing up?

5. What was the most important thing you learned from your parents?

When I was growing up dating was much simpler than today. There was no social media and online dating sites did not exist. My Uncle Frank told me that most girls and boys who worked together farming would develop friendships and sometimes go on dates. It was common for a boy and girl to walk to school together, complete chores with each other and attend church together. Parents were more involved with their children and paid close attention that their sons and daughters dated. Curfews also were common practices by fathers who thought nothing about sending boys home at nightfall.

6. If you liked someone, what would you do when dating them?

7. How does your parent respond to you dating?

8. What were some fun times you remember when growing up in grade school?

_____
_____
_____
_____
_____

Sundays meant family and friends all day long. That day, everybody went to church, Kennon Grove Baptist Church. Reverend Gaines was the pastor. Old Kennon Grove was the hot spot for everybody. The people in the community revered the church, as if God sat in the congregation. Sunday service was a community event.

9. How was religion apart of your life?

_____
_____
_____
_____
_____

10. As a child, what was your fondest memory?

DARK DREARY DAYS

The '30s and '40s were very difficult times for many blacks. It was a very challenging time for families to live, especially in urban communities. During the first quarter of the twentieth century, America journeyed through a dark period on many fronts, socially, economically, politically, and even from a military standpoint. During this period, America struggled to maintain itself and to move forward overall. At the same time, this period also involved the migration period of America. Many southern Americans moved north for industry and for better living than farming or agrarian lifestyles could provide. The North possibly had greater opportunities than the South. Thus, the country began to take flight toward urban industrialization.

But at the same time, America was literally divided between black and white. Blacks were treated as second-class citizens. The lines of separation were both literal and figurative. The opportunities for blacks were not as plentiful and accepted as for the whites. Theaters, restaurants, public transportation systems, professional sports events, educational systems, and religious institutions had sections for blacks only. The nation was segregated. Even the black children in society attended segregated schools. They had to travel miles, oftentimes by foot, to attend school. Few laws were enacted to protect blacks from social abuses, violence, and death. The system in America violated human rights laws. Although the Emancipation Proclamation was issued in 1863, it was not practiced or enacted. Blacks were denied equality.

Numerous events and accounts impacted America and families like the Woods, the Dixons, and millions of others across the country and around the world. One of the major events that occurred was the Great Depression.

> The Great Depression was an economic slump in North America, Europe, and other industrialized areas of the world that began in 1929 and lasted until about 1939. It was the longest and most severe depression ever experienced by the industrialized Western world.
>
> Though the U.S. economy had gone into depression six months earlier, the Great Depression may be said to have begun with a catastrophic collapse of stock-market prices on the New York Stock Exchange in October 1929. During the next three years stock prices in the United States continued to fall, until by late 1932 they had dropped to only about 20 percent of their value in 1929. Besides ruining many thousands of individual investors, this precipitous decline in the value of assets greatly strained banks and other financial institutions, particularly those holding stocks in their portfolios. Many banks were consequently forced into insolvency; by 1933, 11,000 of the United States' 25,000 banks had failed. The failure of so many banks, combined with a general and nationwide loss of confidence in the economy, led to much-reduced levels of spending and demand and hence of production, thus aggravating the downward spiral. The result was drastically falling output and drastically rising unemployment; by 1932, U.S. manufacturing output had fallen to 54 percent of its 1929 level, and unemployment had risen to between 12 and 15 million workers, or 25–30 percent of the work force.[1]

One of the men who lived during the Great Depression was Mr. Mingo, born November 9, 1923, the one brother of Mother Margret. He discussed some of the challenges of living through that era. The blacks coming from the South "were so used to rural living they thought the bathtub was for storing coals." They would heat their apartments by heating up water on a cold stove. They had oil lamps. Most blacks worked as domestics; men labored. Women did hairdressing in their homes. You could smell the hair burning with the hot hair combs.

Mr. Mingo, born November 9, 1923

A lack of jobs persisted, but some blacks had good jobs. If you came from a more affluent family, you worked as Pullman porters and red caps, who worked for the railroad. The red caps had their own homes. Families would tell their daughters to marry red caps. Baggage men told their sons to marry hairdressers. Boys made toys out of little things. If you had skates, you could make a skateboard. You could not afford a bike. Except for the porters, most people were the same. Mrs. Audrey

Mingo's family worked on the railroad. The kids would get food off the train—the uncles would toss food off the train to the kids when passing by. In addition, some of her family worked in a restaurant. They would bring food home.

In the South, many blacks would lay tracks for the railroad. Firemen worked on the train, stuffing coals so the cars could run. If you had a dollar back then, you were good, because it would stretch. Blacks had various trades, but they would get pushed out of the labor jobs. Unions began in the middle '30s. John L. Lewis developed unions because of coal mines. Unions didn't exist before then.[2] People called businessmen *robber barons*, saying they robbed the poor folks. Mr. A. Philip Randolph organized the black porters and established unions.[3]

The second wave of difficulty America experienced was the Great Migration. This occurred for several decades. During the Great Migration, three million blacks moved out of the southern United States to the Northeast, Midwest, and West from 1910 to 1930.[4] African Americans migrated for several reasons. Falling cotton prices brought on an economic depression across the South. Boll weevil insects destroyed much of the cotton crop. Severe floods destroyed the houses and crops of farmers, most of whom were black, along the Mississippi River. Northern industries went through an economic boom, especially as the war in Europe created a demand for war goods. "Those industries could no longer rely on new immigrants from Europe to fill the jobs. The war had limited immigration from Europe. When America got into the war, many young white men (and some young black men) were recruited into the military, leaving their old jobs open. Salaries were higher in the North. Wages in the South ranged from 50 cents to $2 a day. In the North, workers could make between $2 and $5 a day."[5] They also sought to escape the racism and prejudice they experienced in the South.

Some historians differentiate between a First Great Migration (1916–1930), numbering about 1.6 million migrants, and a Second Great Migration, which occurred from 1940 to 1970, in which five million or more people moved to a wider variety of destinations. From 1965 to 1970, fourteen states of the South, especially Alabama, Louisiana, and Mississippi, contributed to a large net migration of blacks to the other three cultural (and census-designated) regions of the United States. By the end of the Second Great Migration, African Americans became an urbanized population. More than 80 percent lived in cities. Fifty-three percent remained in the South, while 40 percent lived in the North and 7 percent in the West.[6] Millions of blacks had left the South looking for new opportunities and searching for a way out of the hardships of the South.

World War II

The third phase of darkness and social and economic turmoil came with World War II. America faced a national crisis, war against other countries and peoples—the Europeans, Germans, and Japanese. It was a critical period for the entire country and even the world. But for blacks, it proved even more difficult. The pattern of racism never ceased. America was not willing to embrace equality for blacks to serve with whites in the military. Blacks served in separate battalions from the white soldiers. One World War II vet, born in 1925, recalled his experience as a youngster in the service. Mr. Roosevelt Alston of Philadelphia, Pennsylvania, married Mrs. Jennie Alston. He was drafted in the service in 1943, two years after the war began.

The war was fought on multiple fronts. The European war with Hitler and the Germans was in progress when war ensued with Japan after the bombing of Pearl Harbor in 1941. The Japanese surprised America in Pearl Harbor; they were not prepared to fight during that period. The Japanese bombed the Americans and killed thousands of soldiers, both black and white. President Roosevelt drafted everyone who could possibly fight, and they went to war. Because of the shortage of manpower, the president needed half as many blacks as whites to be drafted. He forced the army to say that "it would become 10 percent black, giving roughly the same ratio of Negroes to whites that obtained among civilians."[7]

Mr. Alston was stationed in Saipan. He had numerous life-changing encounters both with commanders and during combat. For black soldiers, the difficulty with combat was the Jim Crow system and function ordered them to stay in the background. Many of the commanders and white officers did not want to lead black soldiers. Black soldiers were often reported as victims of violence, especially in the South. Scores got killed or wounded during the war. "Often these casualties resulted from fights between black soldiers and white soldiers and civilians, but even minor violations of local racial codes were punishable by death."[8] As a result of one soldier getting killed by a local police officer in a southern community, race riots and fights between black and white servicemen arose all over the world. This incident and other such situations caused low morale.

"As late as the spring of 1943 only 79,000 out of a total of 504,000 Negro soldiers were overseas because commanders did not want black combats units. The Army solution was to begin converting them to service troops, who were accepted—the more menial the work the better."[9] One commander once stated blacks "have been unable to master efficiently the techniques of modern weapons"; he also denied "the War Department was trying to keep blacks out of combat, though in fact it was."[10] In 1944, the president ordered "the desegregation of all facilities on military posts—an edict that was seldom observed or enforced."[11] As time progressed, some black soldiers were placed in leadership positions.

The actual war—and the actual fighting—challenged Mr. Alston. While he was in Saipan, the American soldiers secured the land, but the Japanese soldiers hid from the American soldiers in the mountains. Occasionally, their snipers would target one of the American soldiers to injury and kill him. Mr. Alston was assigned to defend the American troops and to eliminate that threat. He had fifteen to twenty troops under his command to perform a mission.

One Sunday night, on the way up the mountain, Mr. Alston and his troops quietly ascended to the enemy's area in the dark of night. As he and the soldiers slowly crept up the mountain to fulfill the mission, all of a sudden, one of his soldiers stepped on a dry branch, which alerted the Japanese. Then immediately, a firestorm broke out. The Japanese began firing and throwing hand grenades. Both American and Japanese soldiers were in combat. While this took place, Mr. Alston tried to defend himself in the midst of the battle, but a hand grenade was thrown in his direction. As he went to cover himself on the ground, the hand grenade blew up and hit him in the chest and arms and blew off one of his fingers. Fortunately, he survived the injury.

Mr. Alston was later able to unite with his brother Sam in the service. The Red Cross granted his request to unify him with his family member in the service. In addition, Mr. Alston represented thousands of black soldiers in the military who survived not only an injury but prejudices and discrimination. Other black military groups could endure such racial attacks and understand their role and position, such as the Tuskegee Airmen, air force soldiers who went on many heroic missions for the U.S. Army.[12]

> Although a rigid pattern of racial segregation prevailed in the United States during World War II, nearly 1,000 Black military aviators were trained at an isolated complex near the town of Tuskegee, Alabama, and at Tuskegee Institute. As a result of this "Tuskegee Experiment" 450 Black fighter pilots under the command of Col. Benjamin O. Davis, Jr. fought in the aerial war over North Africa, Sicily, and Europe, flying, in succession, P-40, P-39, P-47, and P-51-type aircraft. These gallant men flew 15,553 sorties completing 1,578 missions with the 12th Tactical, and 15th Strategic, U.S. Army Air Force. Col. Davis later became the first Black general in the U.S. Air Force and rose to the rank of Lt. General.

For every Black pilot there were ten other civilian or military Black men and women on ground support duty. Many of them remained in the military during the post–World War II era and spearheaded the integration of the armed services with the integration into the U.S. Air Force in 1949. Thus the "Tuskegee Experiment" achieved success rather than the expected failure.[13]

Perhaps many of them will not be mentioned. Others in the navy and marines were killed. On occasion, two-thousand-plus blacks were killed during combat, along with thousands of white soldiers. But the black soldiers had to persevere in spite of the internal conflict as well as the external enemy. They were able to rise above the adversity.

Korean Conflict

After World War II, in the late '50s and early '60s, my uncle Frank talked about his role in the military. The family considers him the rock. He was born July 4, 1934. He has been considered a reliable man in the family. He was, and is, the baby boy of the ten siblings, and the sole survivor of the Woods family. At eighteen years of age, he graduated from South Side High School in Newark, New Jersey. He volunteered in the air force. After graduating from high school, he said, "Opportunities for blacks in the services are widening." He trained to become a military police officer during that time. Although the services had segregation, the armed forces became more accepting of blacks after World War II. The black soldiers were treated equally in the service but unaccepted when they returned back home. It seemed its own way of life during that time.

As a soldier, he received his training at Sampson Air Force Base in Syracuse, New York. Later, he was sent to Tampa, Florida, for training as a military police officer. In Florida, black police officers weren't allowed to arrest whites. They had to call for backup from another officer of the same ethnicity to make an arrest. Fortunately, President Eisenhower signed a bill into law for equality, and then blacks could make an arrest equal to their white peers.

During that time, America was involved in what was known as the *Korean conflict*; it wasn't recognized as a major war. America got involved in a peacekeeping mission to ensure safety in various parts of the world. Uncle Frank got relocated to London for a six-month period. He later talked to us about his experience as a military police officer. He stated every day from 2:00 to 3:00 p.m., thousands of citizens would gather in Hyde Park in London to talk about the American people in a negative manner; they talked about the unfair treatment of blacks and ways America abused other ethnic groups. Londoners held this massive community meeting on a daily basis.

In 1962, he was later sent to Puerto Rico. He worked as a military police officer and enjoyed his stay there. The people of Puerto Rico embraced him. He later began a family there. He had a daughter in that country. He stayed for three years.

In 1965, he was stationed in Marrakech, North Africa, which the French government controlled. America's role was to stand by to make sure no wars or other conflicts occurred or to just gather intelligence and information. Uncle Frank told us about two unusual incidents in his stay there. First, the Marrakech men who lived on the mountain would come down into the villages to raid the homes of people who lived in the valley. They would take food, clothes, women, and anything they thought would be useful and then return back into the mountains. Second, the French government would mark the heads of Arab babies born in Marrakech so that the French could identify them to keep them from marrying into their race. Regardless of his feelings about the government's mistreatment or anything else, he stayed committed to his mission to perform his duty for his country in maintaining peace throughout the world.

Uncle Frank later returned home to serve as a police officer and work in the probation department for ten years. Then, he became a police officer in the sheriff's department and in the prosecutor's office in Newark for seventeen years, from the late '50s to the early '60s.

Frank Woods serving in the U.S. Army as a military police officer, Right: Frank Woods, a Newark police officer, in Newark, New Jersey, in the 1960s

Life's most persistent and urgent question is, "What are you doing for others?"

—*Dr. Martin Luther King Jr.*

Discussion Questions & Exercises

Vocabulary Words
Second-Class Citizen
Religious Institution
Laws enacted

Dark Dreary Days

America was literally divided between black and white. Blacks were treated as second-class citizens. The lines of separation were both literal and figurative. The opportunities for blacks were not as plentiful and accepted as the whites. Theaters, restaurants, public transportation systems, professional sports events, educational systems, and religious institutions had sections for blacks only. The nation was segregated. Even the black children in society attended segregated schools. They had to travel miles, often times by foot to attend school. Few laws were in place to protect blacks from social abuses, violence, and death.

In the early 1900's America experienced a myriad of social economic upheavals and tragedies during this period that impacted the world, the community and our families. Some of the families lost loved ones such as husbands, friends, sons, and people in the community. Let's discuss some of your own personal dreary days (your family, experiences, losses, etc.)

1. I remember…

2. How did these situations make you feel?

3. How did you cope with this situation?

4. Have you ever had a racist experience as a youth while growing up? (Please explain)

5. What lessons did your life experiences teach?

TAKING IT TO THE STREETS

During the turbulent '60s, I recall the beginning of the changing of America and the world—the nation was in an upheaval, trying to understand her new role in a diverse society. People were adamant about their freedoms and liberties, unlike previous generations. They took the message to the streets in social protests, marches, and public demonstrations.

This period was known as the civil rights era or movement. Such great men as Dr. Martin Luther King Jr. led it. He stood at the forefront of the Christian or social movement in impacting social policy change to allow blacks and other ethnic groups equal rights and privileges under the law. Certainly, such greats as Malcolm X, representing the Muslim community, heralded a message of equal rights and black empowerment and opportunities for blacks. His approach to equality and fairness under the law uniquely differed from Dr. King's, yet they had similar ambitions. This period of change and social liberties predominately occurred through the religious community. It vocalized unity, harmony, and brotherhood. This message spilled out from the pews and into the streets.

Musical groups urged America and the world to embrace love instead of hate. Men such as the songwriter and musician Marvin Gaye sang songs like "What's Going On." The lyrics to "What's Going On," aimed at men, captured the deep despair and pain of women and the trauma of men in America. The song revealed the brutality and the victimization of our sons and fathers through violent crimes in the streets, racism that plagued our country, and war on foreign soil. Marvin Gaye talked about the search for freedom in his music, emphasizing war wasn't the answer and love was the cure to such chaos and turbulence. In his lyrics, he gave visuals of picket lines of social protests that seemed to frustrate the powers that be. The people needed communication for salvation, but that wasn't the order of the day. He musically articulated the essence of the black movement for social change through radical styles of dress, the Afro, and long hair as means of social protest and identification. This was necessary for a better democracy. Marvin wanted to raise the consciousness in America to what was going on as we grappled with the pursuit of peace, equality, and harmony.

Other musicians such as Bob Marley; Earth, Wind & Fire; and War sang about everyday issues that impacted the world, especially the United States. They were the ambassadors of peace. They gave their messages through music, culture, and the arts. Most of the world sang these songs during this turbulent period in history. Other musical groups like the Beatles also captured the world through song. Others, such as those in the great hippie movement, expressed peace, holding up the peace sign, indicating we as a country wanted peace, not violence. America tried to find her way out of the Vietnam War, social and political unrest, poverty, and miseducation. Racial tension was the theme of both America and most of the world.

With all the social unrest, turbulence, and new emerging communities and values, families like the Woods moved from the South. They eventually left the South, hoping for a better future in the North. By the late '50s and '60s, the Woods family had moved to Newark. All the brothers and sisters moved to begin a new life for themselves. Years later, my grandmother began a church called the House of Love. Along with her brother, she began a church called Cornerstone Baptist Church in Newark, New Jersey.

Reverend Johnny Woods, the pastor of Cornerstone Baptist Church, along with members of the church choir

My mother, Emma Dixon got married, became the wife of James Dixon, and had eight children. Several of my brothers and sisters were born in the South, and the other brothers and sisters were born in Newark. We too had a new beginning. As a kid, I remember living in the projects. My mother sort of functioned similarly to my grandmother. She kept the house in impeccable order. Everything was accounted for—children, food, clothes, and everything else, with seemingly no gaps. She was certainly the boss of the house. She made sure all the "chiren" (or children) did their chores, cleaned the rooms, washed and ironed the clothes, and stayed in order. She would say, "Lord, have mercy. Fix your tie, and tie up your shoes."

The older sisters had responsibility for ensuring the younger brothers and sisters performed their duties. They were second-in-command. It was grievous when my mother left for work because of the sisters' style of authority. We were at the mercy of the sisters, especially us younger twins, me and my twin brother, Carl. We often lost battles because the big sisters were in charge. I always wondered what happened to my older brother Bobby. I would see him at times, but he had lots of friends. He had responsibilities, but I guess he needed a break sometimes because he helped raise the three other sisters and two brothers. I guess it was the sisters' turn to handle or stay involved with raising the rest of my brothers and sisters.

Meanwhile, our mother participated in work that during the early '20s and '30s was called *a day's work*. During that time, period blacks would work for white families to take care of their children and households. They were called *domestic workers*. She did this job almost every day. Somehow, she coordinated a work schedule to clean a family's house and care for its children as if they were her own. She played an incredible role, along with other black women, in nurturing someone else's family while attending to her eight children. Ms. Emma Bell Dixon was a remarkable woman.

I recall the day as a child when I desired to play an instrument: the saxophone. I saw my brother Bob and his band play, so I desired to play an instrument. I didn't know what the instrument was exactly, but I knew the shape. One of my brother Bob's friends said it was the saxophone. So one day, I told my mother what I wanted. She never told me that she aimed to purchase the horn for me, but one day, she came home with a big box. Even to this day, I don't know how she purchased it, but she did.

Somedays, my mother accomplished things that I thought were true miracles. Mothers during that time were seemingly on a mission. Whatever the task, between heaven and hell, she would attain the mission or task. No mountain was high enough to keep her from acquiring food for her young. Some days, our food supply was low. My mother and father were separated. Our father would come over and ensure everybody was safe, but Mom was like a chief; even though Dad was around at times, Mom was the glue. She was a mom who didn't believe in *can't* (not achieving your dreams). She had faith and often said, "The devil is a liar." Thoughts of negativity or unbelief had no place in our lives.

We had a very spiritual family. We had prayer services with the neighbors at least once a week. These were really church services, and all the children had to be mindful of the mothers in charge. Sometimes, my mother would say, "Eat my bread, live under my roof, you gonna do like I say. You gonna go to church." This was like a theme song. "You're gonna do like I say." And if you violated this golden rule of the Dixon family, you were in danger of going not to heaven but the other place. Oh well.

Once a week, my twin brother, Carl, and I challenged the golden rule. On Monday night came the famous *Monday Night Football*. We lived to see that football because we couldn't usually watch football in the afternoon, especially on Sunday, since we were in church from 3:00 p.m. to 6:00 p.m. Although we enjoyed the church, we were seemingly held against our will. What could we do to rebel? Our choices were few to none—all our brothers and sisters were bigger and stronger than us, the uncles were like giants, and the pastor of the church was like the voice of God. We were better off listening than dealing with the consequences.

On Monday nights, the prayer band would come to the house. They would have Bible study. Their children would come along. This was a community meeting. Everybody had to obey the parents or else. (I saw one of the children get slapped. That was the example; if anybody else got out of line, he or she would get it too.) Being young humbled us. We realized the parameters.

One of the greatest moments of my childhood and having a committed mother came the night she didn't seem to have enough food for the children. She prayed, "Oh God, if you would help me, I need food for all my chiren." For some reason, she didn't get compensated that day. So her prayers became evident to her creator. As she road the fifteen-cent bus, she gave out a heartfelt cry to her creator, not knowing how it would happen. Her faith extended beyond her mortal cry. Her petition was just to feed her young. As she exited the bus, with her request made to heaven, and crossed the street, a truck came by, dropping a huge brown package on the ground like a paperboy tossing a newspaper at a customer's door. With curiosity, she peered at the package because it lay before her, with no one near it but her. She approached it as if it might be lethal but also as if it may be the blessing she had hoped for.

She courageously knelt down and touched it. It was something soft wrapped in a huge bag. She became more curious until, finally, she opened the bag. It contained something that smelled like meat. It was just that: fifty pounds of hamburger patties. It was like manna from heaven. Then she beckoned for help. Two men came to her support and brought the food home. We, the children, had beef for weeks: eggs and beef for breakfast, hamburgers for lunch, burgers for snacks, and burgers for dinner. We became the new McDonald's without the arches. Momma Emma was the quintessential mother of faith. Sometimes, she said, "I told Jesus." And oftentimes, she got what she asked for, whether some believed it or not.

Women during the early 1900s were remarkable. They gave a new definition to *womanhood* and *motherhood*. Historically, they nurtured the children of slave masters while attending to their own. Women played the Stella role to support men in achieving their dreams. During and after slavery, their men were often beaten, threatened, abused, and sometimes killed because of the racist white men and systems. Thus, the women had to become their families' backbones. Black women actualized biblical scriptures as helpmates to the men. Historically, African American women always played a vital role in the development of the family and community. Because of the social oppression of her counterpart, the Black male, it was necessary for her to assist in unifying the family. There were numerous laws that denied African Americans their freedom and rights. But, during the post-slavery, reconstruction period, "there were champions such as Mary McLeod Bethune, born in 1875."[14]

She founded the Normal and Industrial School for Young Negro Scholars. McLeod Bethune made the school a center for black and white citizens. In 1923, the college became known as Bethune-Cookman College and she served as the college president until 1947. She initiated numerous women groups, the National Association of Colored Women's Clubs (1924–1928), the National Headquarters for the National Association of Colored Women (1926) and founder and president of the National Council of Negro-Women (1935–1949). She was also a member of the Hoover Committee for Child Welfare and director of the National Business League, the National Urban League and the Commission on Interracial Cooperation, director of the Division of Negro Affairs of the National Youth Administration. She was the first Negro woman to head a federal office and as such she created the informal Black Cabinet of the New Deal.[15]

It was said, many of the women during this period often served in the background to help push men forward in achieving their dreams and aspirations, because of racism that existed. The women conducted numerous events and activities to help men grow and develop, whether through raising monies via chicken dinners to send the pastor to school that they may become educated leaders in the community.

Women like Mary Bethune helped fuel through the black church and assist black men in obtaining their education and pursing their goals in America. The African American church served as a major catalyst for social and political change. First, the church served as a supporter of the signing of the Emancipation Proclamation in 1863. It also functioned as a training ground for intellectual development of both political and religious leadership. During this period, slaves in the South petitioned to legislative bodies of the northern colonies various forms of media to give eloquent voice to the religious conviction that slavery was an abomination before God through ministerial speeches and sermons by independent African Americans anti-slaver tracts, pamphlets and editorials in the first African American newspaper, *Freedom's Journal*.[16]

When I was a kid, my mother always took my brother and sisters to church. On Sundays, Tuesdays, and Fridays, we went to church. Back in those days, the church was hot and exciting; at least our church was. We had hundreds of friends. Kids came from everywhere—New York, Philadelphia, and certainly New Jersey. Our church was electric and inspiring. It had a pulse like New York City. We always had things to do, places to go. Our mother kept us in church. Fortunately, we didn't find it boring. It was the ultimate church for youths and adults; it was a new wave of church. Our lives hinged on the church.

We played sports during the week, and my twin brother and I played in the band and orchestra. Our school had a sixty- to seventy-piece orchestra, which performed a wide range of music, such as Beethoven's Fifth Symphony, other classical pieces, and spiritual music. Moreover, we played in a church big band, with bandstands as if we were on Broadway. I felt like Charlie Parker, infused with Earth, Wind & Fire. The band was hot. My twin brother played the trumpet. We were like a church version of the musical group Kool and the Gang. We wore brightly colored shirts with bow ties, as if we were playing at the Savoy. We contributed this great moment in history to one of the greatest men to ever live, the Reverend Arturo Skinner.

Although the world around us was uncertain and changing, with social uprisings in America and fear and violence in the air, the church maintained her steadfastness once again. Historically, the church was responsible for social and political change in America.

> Prior to the signing of the Emancipation Proclamation the church had its roots deep in the American society. "Pioneers such as Richard Allen became the first bishop of the African Episcopal (AME) Church. Allen had separated from the white Christian Church because of practices of discrimination. The movement of the African American Church began to thrust forward during the 1800s and emerged as a renowned institution. The AME Church was at the forefront of social change and equality.
>
> It was the AME Church that spearheaded organized protest. Anti-slavery resolutions were passed in the North by the new AME and AME Zion denomination while local churches served as stations of the Underground Railroad. The "churchmen," as they were called, generally, were the best educated African Americans. They furnished leadership in the churches and in the community. The most predominant orators and activists, Harriet Tubman, Sojourner Truth and Frederick Douglass, were all products of the African American Church.
>
> Douglass was a premier leader and preacher from the AME Zion Church and was a major participant in the abolitionist movement. In addition to Douglass's role in the movement was Henry Highland Garnet, a Presbyterian." [17]

The church gave birth to other local leadership that became international in scope. Some of these leaders, unlike Dr. King and Malcolm X, didn't have national status, but we can recognize them as pioneers in the African American church and community. The Reverend Dr. Arturo

Skinner was a contemporary of Dr. King and Malcolm X. People said during that era, you were either a Skinner Ike or a Muslim Ike. Reverend Skinner commanded respect through extraordinary leadership. He came from the next generation of the Pentecostal movement, or the school of the Reverend Charles Mason that brought the Azusa Street Revival to America during the early twentieth century. Reverend Mason played an instrumental role in revitalizing the church, giving men and women in the African American community and other ethnic groups a new sense of hope for the present and the future.

But the Reverend Arturo Skinner gave the church a spiritual makeover. He brought glitz and glitter to the church, a Broadway flair to the pews and seats. We can view him as a catalyst for the faith movement in America. His life story unfolded in an incredible fashion. His biography breathes insight into his earlier years before his conversion, spending money and chasing women on Broadway. He was viewed as a man of the nightlife, entertainment, and dance. People stated he abused drugs and alcohol. At his lowest point, after his mother's death, he was on the road to suicide, and at his turning point, he had a spiritual encounter while anticipating to jump in front of a train at a Brooklyn, New York, station. He heard a voice say, "If you turn around, you will be one of today's greatest mouthpieces to the world." He went into a new business in serving God.

After overcoming the drug habit, Reverend Skinner began to reconnect with family members and meet new friends. On his journey to become a minister, he attended the Bethel Bible Institute in Jamaica Queens. He enrolled in an accelerated program and began to study the Bible. He submerged himself in studying and developing a spiritual relationship with God. He modeled and shaped himself for his greater ministry and the world.

Although Reverend Skinner was self-motivated and driven, he benefited from an extended community of support networks; numerous mothers surrounded and nurtured him. In New York City, a mother named Violet Watson took him in to live in her home. He did chores and earned his keep. He served as a loving son to Mother Watson and as a brother to Barbara, Grace, and James Watson, Mother Watson's adult children. Other mothers joined in support of this great man, such as Mother Emma Futch . And finally a Polish mother, Amrtys, faithfully prayed and uplifted Reverend Skinner in Newark, New Jersey. She provided Reverend Skinner with food and shelter in his growth process. This was where the Deliverance Evangelistic movement began.

Deliverance Evangelistic Center at 505 Central Avenue in Newark, New Jersey, Top Right: Reverend Dr. Arturo Skinner hosting an international crusade at Madison Square Garden in New York City, 1973, Bottom Left: The Deliverance Band performing at the Deliverance Temple in Newark, New Jersey, Bottom Right; Reverend Arturo Skinner at Madison Square Garden, showing enthusiasm and ambition

The stage was set and the curtains were drawn for this spiritual giant. In the 1960s, the Deliverance Evangelistic Church began to emerge throughout the United States and the world. The Deliverance Evangelistic Center had its headquarters located in Newark, New Jersey, at 505 Central Avenue. It had 2,000 enrolled members in the congregation attending on a weekly basis. In addition, a church in Brooklyn, New York, accommodated at least 1,500 members on DeKalb Avenue. Other churches existed in Philadelphia, which Reverend Skinner frequented every week to minister to hundreds and thousands. Each week, he ministered to a minimum of four to five thousand people. He was one of the first African American men to conduct a crusade at Madison Square Garden in New York City. Approximately ten-thousand-plus people attended.[18]

In 1971, Reverend Skinner purchased the Deliverance Evangelistic Center headquarters temple at 621 Clinton Avenue in Newark. The temple accommodated approximately 2,500 people. It was always packed to capacity. He had a host of ministries, such as ones for education and cultural arts, youth development, music and recreation, and outreach programs. They included the following: Bible institute, bookstore, Boy Scouts, businessmen's fellowship, crusade choir, crusade team, day camp, deacons and deaconesses board, deliverance recording, *Deliverance Voice* magazine, education department, Girl Scouts, junior Voices of Deliverance, missionaries and mother board, men's ministry, orchestra and band, prayer staff, prison outreach, radio outreach, Sunday school, trustees, ushers, five-hundred-voice choir, volunteers, willing workers, young choir, and many more.

Throughout his ministry, Reverend Skinner always extended a helping hand with a heart of love and concern to the needy. He made sure the young were properly and appropriately sheltered and provided for their needs, to the extent he provided food and clothing to them and paid their parents' rent and utility bills as needed. He provided tuition for many young people to go to the college of their choice. In the summer, he provided youths with jobs. We saw money come out of his pockets. All year long, it was like Christmas for most of the children and families. They had a remarkable resource and a king among them.

He was one of the world's greatest ministers during the radical '60s era. He was certainly a village leader to millions of people and an inspiration and influence to youths across the world. He was the true light and angel during the past that impacted the present. He was a man of purpose, vision, and passion for humanity; a voice of God; and a modern-day apostle. He established more than sixty-five Deliverance Evangelistic Centers throughout the United States, Trinidad, Barbados, Africa, India, England, Mexico, and Puerto Rico and an orphanage in Haiti.

I recall when I was a child, Reverend Skinner took our family and hundreds of other kids on social outings to crusades, dinners, and amusement parks. He was the epitome of a pastor. He would purchase clothes for the kids and families, concerned about the widowed, fatherless, misfortunate, sick, lame, and outcast. I'll never forget when I graduated from high school in 1976 and Reverend Skinner told me and my twin to find and select our graduation suits. He would take the tab of and pay the cost for the suits. My brother Carl and I went to New York and purchased the two tops suits and pairs of shoes in the store. When we returned to tell him, he called us *big spenders* and gave us the money for the graduation suits. We were blessed beyond measure, not only us but most of our friends who had good report cards. If you didn't have good grades or treat your parents right, you would be doomed and punished. But those of us who obeyed our parents and strived to be decent children benefited.

Reverend Skinner invested in the youths and families of the church and community. He passed away in 1976, prior to our graduation, but his legacy will live on forever. He was a pioneer and one of the world's greatest men to ever live.

> *Women have been endowed with the power of influence and men have been endowed with the power of authority.*
>
> —*Anonymous*

Discussion Questions & Exercises

Word/Character Identification
Turbulent
Adamant
Upheaval
Chaos
Methodology
Advocating

Dr. King
Malcolm X
Mary McLeod Bethune
Richard Allen
Rev. Arturo Skinner
Bishop Charles Mason/ Azusa Street Revival

Taken it to the Streets

The message of take it to the street represented a period in history of social action and protest. People became extremely vocal about situations and issues happening in the community. This was a turbulent **time;** it was the beginning of America and the world changing—the nation was in an upheaval, trying to understand her new role in a diverse society. People were adamant about their freedoms and liberties, unlike previous generations. People took the message to the streets in social protests, marches, and public demonstrations. This period was known as the Civil Rights era. Great men such as Dr. Martin Luther King Jr. led this movement. He stood at the forefront of the Christian or social movement, impacting social policy change allowing blacks and other ethnic group's equal rights and privileges under the law. Another great man, Malcolm X who represented the Muslim community, heralded a message of equal rights and black empowerment. He demanded that Blacks should have similar opportunities as Whites. His approach to equality and fairness under the law uniquely differed from Dr. Kings philosophy, yet they had similar ambitions. This period of change and social liberties predominately occurred through the religious community. It vocalized unity, harmony, and brotherhood. This message spilled out from the pews and into the streets.

1. What was Dr. King's over-all message?

2. What was Malcolm X message?

3. Did Dr. King and Malcolm X have a similar approach addressing community issues?

4. Rev. Arturo Skinner was one of the local leaders in the Newark Community during the 60's to 70's, who are some of the people you know advocating for families and communities today?

    b. What is their role and position/title?

    c. What did they do to help their communities?

5. What was the benefits overall?

6. What are some of the important issues that we contend with in our communities today?

7. What issues should we deal with more or give more voice to in the present?

8. How could you or others become proactive in social matters?

9. What role did the religious community play in our community during the civil rights era?

10. Does the religious community today continue to play the same role as it did during the Civil Rights era?

DON'T OPEN THE DOOR

Living in the projects with seven brothers and sisters—Bobby, Arzelia, Original, Margie, Jerry, Edward, and the youngest, Carl—was like an amusement park that never closed. I had a life of adventure even in crises on any given day. As children, I guess we would have been classified as economically impoverished or simply poor. But socially and spiritually, we were the wealthiest family on the block. On a normal day, we had family dinner after work, where we would gather at the dinner table and talk about our day, or went to school during the day. All the family members had chores or responsibilities: doing homework, cleaning the apartment, cooking, or something.

Our apartment was decorated as if we lived in a plush penthouse; we had beautiful red and white curtains and carpeted floors throughout the apartment. It was prettier than all our neighbors' apartments. Eighty to one hundred families lived in one building, and perhaps twenty buildings stood in close proximity. Every now and then, family rivalries arose; one family would fight another family.

Three sisters: Arzelia (beside Valarie Martin, a family friend), Margie, and Original

Monday night was prayer night. It was bigger than *Monday Night Football*. The mothers in the neighborhood would have four to five families gathered together for a prayer meeting. Each mother would bring at least two to four children to the meeting. I never knew how we had enough room for everyone. It was standing room only. It was like a revival service in the house. Everyone had to attend prayer night; if you didn't, you were doomed. (Your parents may immediately send you to the hot place—and if not sent there, you would want to go there because you would likely get smacked or hit with a shoe.)

Once in a while, my twin brother, Carl, and I would try to stay in the back room to watch *Monday Night Football*, but my mother would come into the room, hit the television off switch, and run us into the living room, sometimes with a shoe. Back then, your parents would discipline you by any means—whippings, slaps, shoes, belts, brooms, or any other way possible. Discipline came like a judge saying, "Order in the court." (We had seemingly very few choices.)

This was our community fellowship and social network. We expressed our testimonies. We shared our pains but prayed for another day of blessings. We sang songs like "Sweet Hour of Prayer" and other great spiritual songs, like "Just Another Day That the Lord Has Kept Me," "Real, Real, Jesus Is Real to Me," "There Is Power in the Blood," and others. We were wealthy beyond measure because of the love we experienced. Every now and then, we experienced an emergency. The lights or the power in the building would go out. We lived on the sixth floor, and with the lights out, it was impossible to go upstairs without running into someone or the walls. But someway, somehow, my momma, Emma B., had a way and a plan to get her children upstairs safe, out of darkness. When we got outside, we would call for her to come to the window. She would say, "Wait a minute," and then come to the window with a newspaper and matches. We would then proceed upstairs, after we lit the newspaper with a match. It was like a burning torch. It's a miracle we didn't get burned to death.

We filled our days with adventure. My father would come by the house and make sure we didn't get out of line or misbehave. Our mother and father were separated, but he wasn't too far away or unreachable. One of my fondest memories of our father is the time we went shopping. In the beginning of September, our father asked what Carl and I wanted him to buy us just before we would return to school after the summer. With joy and elation, we replied, "A football suit." And amazingly, he consented to our request. We entered the heaven of all heavens. We thought we were now ready for the NFL; we felt as if we were joining the NFL. My twin selected the Green Bay Packers uniform, and I selected the New York Giants uniform. Add to that all the accessories: shoulder pads, kneepads, and cleats. If we had a call from the NFL, we would go through the television if it was possible.

With exuberance, we returned home to get ready for our junior football game on the playground to show off our uniforms. Suddenly, our mother came into the house from working. She asked us what our father got us to wear. Well, with enthusiasm, we said, "A football suit." We danced as if we had just got a touchdown.

Our mother replied as if we had stepped out of bounds. She said, "You can't wear a football suit to school. You need clothes to wear." Our vision for reaching the NFL from the projects just got smaller. We had to return the suits. It felt as if our touchdown was reversed. Later, we obtained other football suits.

Four brothers playing sports, Edward, Jerry, Carl, and Charles

Family life was always full of episodes, just like in the movies. We played on the large playground almost every day. I loved running, racing, and playing sports. I had kids to play with all the time along with my brothers. Most of these kids came from single-family households. The mothers were hard workers. They went to work and sent their kids to school to learn. If they had discipline problems with their kids in school, oh boy, those kids had hell to pay. They just knew their time had come for a beat-down or whipping.

During that time, teachers could discipline or reprimand you and your neighbors. Teachers would tell you to put your hands out, and then they would whack you with a ruler. Then, if your neighbors saw you acting out, the teacher would either physically whack you or tell your mother. There was no rest for the contrary or unruly. And in high school, the discipline could get even worse; a teacher would hit you in the butt with a giant paddleboard. (Where was the Division of Youth and Family Services then? Smiling.)

Even though many of these families struggled, they had moral and spiritual values that kept them moving forward. That period had hundreds of single families. In 1936, 147,000 families in America received welfare. It grew to five million in 1994, from less than 1 percent to 15 percent of families receiving welfare (with welfare reform occurring four years later). "Between 1963 and 1973, there was a striking 230 percent increase—not because of a bad economy (unemployment was actually quite low during most of this period) nor simply because of an increase in family breakdown (both divorce and illegitimacy were rising, though not nearly as fast as the welfare caseload)."[19] The increase was due to the results of programmatic changes that made it easier for income-eligible families to get benefits. More than 90 percent of welfare recipients were single females.

Oftentimes, our mother would say, "Don't open the door." Initially, we thought she said it to protect us from harm or strangers. But as time went on, we discovered welfare workers would just drop by to see if our father or a male partner lived in the house. If they discovered the man lived there, it would jeopardize the mother's benefits. Often, the women in our community wouldn't allow their boyfriends or spouses to stay at the apartment in fear of their welfare benefits being cut.

Although living in the projects had its rewards, it also had its perils. On occasion, men would accompany older women on the elevators. They would ride with them and then steal their pocketbooks. Having a big family reduced your liability. Every now and then, a family member was challenged—not for a long period of time. Nevertheless, as we continued to reside there, our family witnessed a misfortune that eventually became a blessing. One Sunday, while attending church with the family, our mother was summoned to leave church immediately in the middle of service because our apartment that we loved so much was on fire. As all seven of us left church, we were filled with anxiety. One of the church members drove us home.

As we got closer, we saw the fire truck at the apartment building. Nervously, we ran out of the car, and we saw hoses coming from the truck all the way upstairs. The building's hallway lights were out. The elevator wasn't working. Everything in the building was dark, and the floor leading up to the sixth floor was covered with water. As we approached our floor and the apartment, we saw the walls charred with black smoke. Our beautiful curtains and the five-hundred-dollar stereo were burned. Everything seemingly was destroyed.

We were then forced to move out. It filled us with grief. We moved in with our grandmother and later moved into another building for several months, and later, my brother Bob went to Vietnam and obtained a GI Bill. We were then ready to start life anew. We moved to East Orange, New Jersey.

> *Cowardice asks the question, "Is it safe?" Expediency asks the question, "Is it politic?" ... But, conscience asks the question, "Is it right?" And there comes a time when one must take a position that is neither safe, nor politic, nor popular, but one must take it because one's conscience tells one that it is right.*
>
> —*Dr. Martin Luther King Jr.*

Discussion Questions & Exercises

Vocabulary Words/Character Identification
GI Bill
Vietnam War

Don't Open the Door

The mothers in the neighborhood would have four to five families gathered together for spiritual and community support meetings. Each mother would bring at least two to four children to the house meetings.

1. Have you participated in any spiritual support meetings?

    If so, explain your experience?

2. What recreational activities did your family participate in?

3. What was one of your fondest memories growing up with your family?

4. Did your parents ever talk about moral or spiritual values, i.e.. "Love your neighbor as yourself or treat your neighbors and friends with respect?"

5. Was public assistance common in your family or community (welfare or perhaps homelessness)?

6. What do you think about people (poor or homeless families) receiving public assistance, or homeless families?

WHO'S AT THE DOOR? THE VIETNAM WAR

One of my greatest influences of my youth was my oldest brother, Bob. He was a great pianist and karate practitioner. I enjoyed his creative abilities. As a kid, I watched him perform piano pieces such as jazz, classical, and Latin music or whatever else—songs like "Maple Leaf Rag," urban songs like "The Ghetto" by Donny Hathaway, and other great ones written during that time. Furthermore, he performed with a musical group called OCHO when living in the projects. They were a Latin band. I enjoyed the horn players. They inspired me to play the sax as a kid. Living in the projects was the training ground to the rest of my life.

Bob was like Bo Jackson, the great sports athlete, in that he could do anything and everything. He was a nonconformist. He was, or is, a person who explored the world through reading, visiting places locally most people may not have dared to explore. For a period, Bob was not in our family's midst on a daily basis. In 1965, Bob graduated from Arts High School. He remained socially conscious of what happened in society. He saw a broad scope of society through his educational and personal experiences and his personal interests. He was at one of his highest points of learning about the world.

In his local encounters, he experienced the riots in Newark and across the nation. People fought and looted; buildings burned down. "Newark was one of several cities across the country where riots broke out in the late 1960s. Years of poverty and discrimination had created a powder keg of frustration in many black communities. ... Stores were looted and some were burned down. After a policeman was killed, the governor sent in the National Guard with orders to use their weapons at will. ... The National Guard used tanks and armored vehicles to block off streets, keeping people from entering the city."[20]

He recalls men like Amiri Baraka, a community and social activist. Bob could relate to social activists because of the injustices toward blacks and families in black America. He also embraced men like Malcolm X, as he understood the plight of African American people. The '60s were a turbulent period. Numerous social groups and organizations fought for equality and justice, as did religious groups, like Muslims or the Nation of Islam and people of the Christian faith. Other groups like the hippies were after peace and harmonious living.

The hippie subculture developed as a youth movement that began in the United States during the early 1960s and spread around the world. Its origins can be traced back to classical culture and to European social movements in the early twentieth century. "From around 1967, its fundamental ethos—including harmony with nature, communal living, artistic experimentation particularly in music, and the widespread use of recreational drugs—spread around the world."[21] Then radical groups embraced more aggressive means of equality, like the Black Panthers. They believed in an eye for an eye. They would resort to violence, if necessary, because of the violent times of racism. Gangs like the Young Lords and the Blackstone Rangers of Chicago grew.

These all influenced Bob prior to his high school graduation. In the midst of this social upheaval, the Vietnam War became part of the social fabric of the country and world. Thousands upon thousands of young men went to war at seventeen or eighteen years of age and sometimes illegally and younger. Some of these young men prepared for war and were drafted. Bob prepared for war through his class with a teacher named Ms. Novac. She cared about the students. She introduced the students to world books on communism and the French Revolution by Charles Dickens, and other books like James Baldwin's *The Fire Next Time* and *Notes of a Native Son*. Bob was exposed to the world through his high school education. Black students had great consciousness they would fight other races of people. But some men helped propel the spirit of unity in the community toward blacks, such as Mr. Ruban Johnson, a science teacher at Arts High School. Bob was very fond of him and inspired by his passion for African American people.

Bob Dixon, when he was a student at Arts High School in Newark, New Jersey, in 1968, Right: Bob Dixon, as a soldier in the Vietnam War (1968–1970), with his watchdog

On February 26, 1968, Bob was drafted into the U.S. Army. My mother tried to keep him from going into the service. She got in contact with the army, stating he was the sole supporter of the family because our father didn't reside in the home, but to no avail. He still got recruited. The most agonizing experience was the entire draft process. At the recruitment office, one had to sign up for the service and then receive a letter in the mail. It was stated many family members cried for their sons as they left for the service. Obviously, they didn't have a choice on whether they could stay. Most young men got recruited, except if you were in school, you got excused from service. However, Bob wasn't as fortunate in that regard. On the same day he signed up, Bob was drafted and sent to another location—Fort Dix in Trenton, New Jersey. His journey to Vietnam began. He stated he felt numb or tranquilized.

After the bus from Newark to Dix, the training academy, the first day of duty involved getting familiar with day-to-day operations and functions in the armed forces. The next activities were really just to dive into the routine of becoming a soldier. Each soldier went through these steps.

1. First, he got a haircut; everyone got a Caesar or a bold haircut.

2. Next, he got a physical examination.

3. After that, he got a change of clothing, his army uniform.

4. He was assigned to his barracks, along with his platoon members.

5. Finally, he learned to march in step and the army protocol (saying, "Yes, sir," "No, sir," "Attention," and so on).

The army sergeants would harass the soldiers with demanding commands that they had to obey or else suffer the consequences. When the sergeants said to jump, run, or whatever, they had to comply.

Bob was assigned to the engineering company to build roads. After several months in training, he received his orders to go to Vietnam. He and other soldiers flew to Seattle, Washington. They had a four-day layover. Later, they traveled to Hawaii and then to the Philippines. Finally, he landed in Vietnam. The war that the media publicized, with its casualties, deaths, and injuries, was now before his eyes. Statistics record the amount of deaths in the Vietnam War: "One out of every 10 Americans who served in Vietnam was a casualty. 58,169 were killed and 304,000 wounded out of 2.59 million who served. Although the percent who died is similar to other wars, amputations or crippling wounds were 300 percent higher than in World War II. 75,000 Vietnam veterans are severely disabled."[22]

As the plane landed in Cam Ranh Bay and the door opened, the men anxiously waiting, an intense heat emerged like hot steam from an oven, perhaps 105 degrees. It had a stench like chemicals burning. For three to four days, he could not use the bathroom or release his bowels, perhaps because of nerves, the food, anxiety about war, or all the above reasons. They stayed in Cam Ranh at a military base. During the day and night, military fires went on. A bomb could travel five miles to hit a target.

Days later, his platoon went on a convoy to the central highlands in the mountains, nothing but bare lands. They bunked there—they had to set up camp. The only place they could go to the bathroom was in the woods. Some of the platoon members got shot or even killed at times in building roads. They saw death all around them. They had to always stay away from the shooting zone; sometimes, innocent people died because of their ignorance of this territory.

One of the worst experiences Bob encountered came one day when going into Cam Ranh village. He had just passed a pickup truck with civilians on it, and after several seconds, forty to fifty feet away from him, came a loud explosion. The people in the truck next to him were crushed to death, and bodies lay all over the road. He was fortunate. He counted down his days of duty. He later stayed in Vietnam for a year. Soon, he was deployed back to the United States of America.

It was a sunny day in the projects. Then a knock came at the door. Our family stayed involved in our usual activities, but then a different kind of knock came, with authority, and a familiar voice along with it, saying to open the door. It was loud and aggressive. With curiosity, we answered again, "Who's at the door?" Then again, "Who's at the door?" With hearts racing, the family shouted, "Who's at the door?" My mother screamed, cried, and yelled at the top of her voice because we hadn't heard from him for a long period of time. We hadn't heard from him in months. We didn't know if he was dead or alive. Vietnam War's casualties came out every day.

It certainly turned out to be a happy day. Sister Margie said she dreamed he had a guardian angel—a dog. Later, our family moved to East Orange. It was refreshing. God made a way for Momma Emma and the "chiren."

> *The first question which the priest and the Levite asked was: "If I stop to help this man, what will happen to me? But ... the Good Samaritan reversed the question: "If I do not stop to help this man, what will happen to him?"*
>
> *—Dr. Martin Luther King Jr.*

Discussion Questions & Exercises

Vocabulary Words/Character identification
Hippies
Amiri Baraka
Young Lords
Blackstone Rangers
Black Panthers
James Baldwin's The Fire Next Time/ Notes of a Native Son
Brown vs Board of Education

Who's at the Door?

1. Who was your greatest inspiration growing up, i.e. a Superman, A Jazz musician, Vocalist, etc..?

   Spankings or whippings were a way of discipline or a part of our culture during this period. The bible stated "spare the rod, spoil the child". Parents would discipline you by any means—whippings, slaps, shoes, belts, or brooms. Discipline came like a judge demanding, "Order in the court."

2. Do you think we should still use this style of discipline?

3. What role did the Nation of Islam or Muslims play during the 60's.

4. What was the Hippie's movement in America?

5. During the 60's the military issued the draft for young people to go to war, how would you feel about being drafted?

Bob Dixon a soldier in the Vietnam War, 1968 – 1970, with his watch Dog

THE MEN'S MOVEMENT

The '70s and '80s were an interesting period. For half my adult life, I've worked with males and young fathers. Over the years, my passion for working with men and families has intensified. I guess I understand working in one field oftentimes can lead to boredom or burnout, but for me, my interest in the issues and subject of engaging males has only heightened. For twenty-five years plus, I have been engaged in comprehending the social, emotional, physical, and spiritual issues of males or men.

As a community program support advocate, I've worked with males in a fathers-based program for years. During this period, we began to recognize the important roles of men and fathers in our community. In the 1980's and 1990's, the concept of a fatherhood program was nothing but a whisper. A person named Dr. Linda Jones introduced the fatherhood concept to the city of Newark. At the time, the community agencies and hospital and health-care services were geared toward mothers and children. Countless programs for women were available. On the other hand, the services for men were almost nonexistent. Men were seemingly ousted from the social services system network, perhaps because of the notion they could tough it out or handle any situation. Perhaps war, incarceration, unemployment, and other social factors could be attributed to men not being included in the family structure.

But we could describe the '70s as the period we reached the promised land. America had a new rhythm and dance. We had disco fever, through "The Hustle," "Stayin' Alive," and "Y.M.C.A." We had reached a period of liberation. America was alive and well. Civil rights laws were now established; men and women shared equal rights. Blacks were no longer second-class citizens by law. They had the rights to vote and ride in the front or back of the bus. Society had resurrected the laws of the Emancipation Proclamation along with the amendment for blacks to receive equal treatment under the Constitution of the United States.

That was a great time for the African American community. Certainly, many black leaders of that time celebrated their accomplishments, but they had to mourn the losses of some of their advocates and champions for equal rights, like Dr. Martin Luther King Jr., Malcolm X, and President Kennedy. They were the true heroes. America experienced a new surge of momentum moving forward in enforcing laws of equality, providing blacks with new opportunities in society overall. More black politicians emerged, and students attended school through the Civil Rights Act of the '60s. The case of *Brown v. Board of Education* brought a new spirit throughout the land, in American radio and television, and throughout the world regarding the freedoms and rights of civil liberties.

New television shows such as *Miami Vice* were cool and stylish. It showed blacks and whites working together in Hollywood. Other black sitcoms and comedies started, like *Sanford and Son*, about a single father raising his son in an impoverished residential setting. Then came *Good Times*, showing blacks living in the projects and struggling to live the American dream but having strong family values. As for women in America, new roles came on TV shows like *Charlie's Angels* and *Laverne & Shirley*. Women's roles on television became sexier. The pre-'60s' long dresses and sleeves vanished, with a new fashionable style. Women's roles were redefined. Women were no longer passive housewives following whatever the man or father said as the law. The notion that *father knows best* got tossed to the wind in mainstream America. Women began to reposition themselves in society in more of a leadership capacity.

In this post-'60s era, after the women's movement burned their bras, the fathers and men in families declined, especially in urban communities. Dr. Jawanza Kunjufu, a social and economic scientist, stated, "From 1910 there has been a decline in fathers living in the homes in the African American community. 90% of children had their fathers home. In the 1960s the figure dropped slightly to 80% and in each decade it declined by at least 10%. ... In the 90s the figure declined to 38%."[23] The momentum behind women becoming independent and progressive in society reached an all-time high. Women became more visible in the workforce in nontraditional roles, such as in corporate America industries that normally wouldn't accept them. As a society, we seemingly turned the corner from men being the heads of households. Female heads of households became commonplace.

For decades, women fought for their rights. In the '20s, they fought for the right to vote, and in the '60s, women fought for respect and to be taken seriously. In the '20s, we watched women abandon conservative styles of dress to become more sexually explicit. They wore makeup, cut their hair short, and began to smoke in public. Moreover, they received the right to vote; the Nineteenth Amendment created a new era for women. However, the 1960s propelled the women's movement to an entirely new level. That was the era of feminism. It gave way to new fashion, such as miniskirts, fishnet stockings, beads, headbands, and boots. During that period, the governor established a commission to provide equal opportunities for women. It was in the '60s that women started to work outside the home.

But this period also created social turmoil or a sexual revolution. The numbers of cases of sexual assault and domestic violence increased. The crime of rape increased in numbers.[24] It sparked the development of the birth control pill. Women began advocacy groups and organizations, such as the National Organization for Women (NOW), founded by

Betty Friedan and Reverend Pauli Murray, the first African American Episcopal priest. Ms. Betty Friedan became the president of NOW. The group dealt with issues such as work discrimination, harassment in the workplace, justice systems, secure abortions, birth control and reproductive rights for all women, an end to violence against women, and eradication racism, sexism, and homophobia, promoting equality and justice.[25]

The new roles for women seemed to awaken a new era in American culture. Women didn't have to rely on a spouse to support them and to maintain a family as once upon a time. On the other hand, the editorials for men said just the opposite. Men seemingly lost ground educationally, economically, socially, and spiritually. Fathers left their families at high rates, as mentioned. "Papa Was a Rollin' Stone" perhaps became the theme for the post-'60s. The fabric of the family had shifted, and not in favor of father heads of households. In almost every capacity, the roles of fathers and men declined. Year by year, the social stamina of men in the community eroded.

By 1980, numerous articles and reports covered the diminishing black families. One in particular was "The Vanishing Family: Crisis in Black America," which aired in 1986. This portrayed the rise of single-parent-family households and many of the issues in the black family. Statistics revealed, "Half of all black (female) teen-agers become pregnant. ... In the black inner city practically no teen-age mother gets married. ... The leading cause of death for young black men is murder. One in 21 will be killed before the age of 25. ... Nearly half of young men in the inner city are arrested before they reach 18."[26]

An organization and a movement began to emerge to try to head off the atrocities of this fatherless surge in America. Two distinct groups emerged. The first group or social movement that began was the Promise Keepers. This group was not aimed at a particular ethnic group because fatherlessness was a factor and problem in almost every household in America. Bill McCartney, then the head football coach of the University of Colorado Boulder, founded the Promise Keepers in 1990. He envisioned using his home football stadium Folsom Field as a gathering place for training and teaching on what it meant to be godly men. Their mission declared that the "Promise Keepers is a Christ-centered ministry dedicated to uniting men through vital relationships to become godly men who influence their world."[27] The group quickly grew from humble beginnings, earning the support of Jerry Falwell, Pat Robertson, and Focus on the Family's James Dobson.

In July 1990, seventy-two men met at Boulder Valley Christian Church in Boulder to organize what would become the Promise Keepers' first event at the University of Colorado Events Center. From that point on, the Promise Keepers' membership gradually grew. Approximately 4,200 members attended the first official Promise Keepers conference in July 1991. The organization was incorporated as a nonprofit in the state of Colorado in December. In their later years, they would raise close to $100 million through this initiative. They were "famous for packing football stadiums with their emotional, men-only rallies." They held a large rally on the National Mall in Washington, DC. It was stated this march contained more people than the Million Man March in 1995.

But "the Promise Keepers' growth was not without incident, however—critics attacked the group's ties to the religious right-wing establishment, its championing of male-dominated family structures, and McCartney's advocacy of anti-gay legislation as well as his ties to the radical pro-life group Operation Rescue."[28] They would host large events in stadiums to assist men in prioritizing their responsibilities and reconnecting their families. This multiethnic campaign lasted several years.

The second movement was the Million Man March, initiated through the Muslim religion, which engaged participation from the black church rally and the black community toward responsibility and change. The Million Man March captured the attention of America, unlike Dr. King's march on Washington. It gave voice to the civil rights movement. This march was designed to fortify and strengthen the black male or men's role in society and remind black men of their moral, ethical responsibility to their families and community.

On October 16, 1995, the day of the Million Man March, the *Home News Tribune* interviewed me, Mr. Charles Dixon, community activist, along with three prominent African American leaders in the community. They came from across the state of New Jersey: Mr. David Harris, executive director of the Greater New Brunswick Day Care Council; Reverend Donald Hillard, pastor of the Second Baptist Church in Perth Amboy, New Jersey; and Mr. Harry Russell, retired director of Mental Health Services at Robert Wood Johnson University Hospital. The interviewer asked us about the significance of the Million Man March. All the panelists supported the march but had different views on how to achieve the vision of unity in the African American community. Reverend Donald Hillard stated he supported the Million Man March and vehemently opposed the ideology, philosophy, and theology of the religion and group that sponsored the event, but the event was larger than the sponsor of another faith.

Some of the excerpts from the conversation are as follows.[29]

> Hillard: The media wanted to shift the march from black pain to white anxiety or to focus on religion. But instead we are bringing leaders together on a small level, 1,000 black men come together once a year—through a rites-of-passage program. Men's fellowship programs operate on a regular basis. It may have a hundred youth and young men in attendance. This is happening with churches across the nation, irrespective to denomination because all of us see a consistent dismantling of protection from government and repeal of civil right laws and a continual historical pattern of a society stepping on the heads of the African American community, primarily the African American male.

Russell: There are not only minorities. There are other kids who are in serious trouble. And my concern is if we come up with "this is what the black community is doing," people get angry: they get jealous, not realizing that we're all supposed to be going at the same pace. There are people who migrated here and I can count them, different ethnic groups, and they come in and they achieve. Why is it that this group hasn't been able to do that? It isn't that we don't have the ability. The black American is the only immigrant group to this country for other than the two Es: economics and education. It is the only group that was systematically family fragmented ... the only group, during slavery, that was politically forced to distrust one another, distrust between the field and house.

Mr. Harris, quoting from a book of essays by Richard Wright, titled *12 Million Black Voices*: "We black folk, our history and our present being, are a mirror of all the manifold experiences of America. What we want, what we represent, what we endure is what America *is*. If we black folk perish, America will perish. If America has forgotten her past, then let her look into the mirror of our consciousness and she will see the *living* past." Essentially, what he is saying here is the differences between black folk or white folk is not blood or color, and the ties that bind us are deeper than those that separate us.

Russell: There is a concerted effort for a unified group of people in a way that I have not experienced in my lifetime to come together and relate about experiences and about how to improve.

Dixon: Many of the young men in our community have low self-esteem. Our goal is to help them improve their self-worth or -image. They come from single-female heads of households, they don't often see positive male role models in the home. This march will be an inspiration for many of them, especially seeing older men at the forefront.

Russell: We have a united front moving together and realize a better life for everybody. We are all in this together and it is okay for me to move up and to take charge alongside [white leadership] or if not beside, then in front of.

If a man hasn't discovered something that he will die for, he isn't fit to live.

—Dr. Martin Luther King Jr.

Discussion Questions & Exercises

Vocabulary Words/ Character Identification
Eradication
Sexism,
Homophobia
Feminism
Hippies
Civil Rights Act of the '60s
Promise Keepers
Million Man March
Richard Wright

THE MEN'S MOVEMENT

Often, young fathers have numerous issues and concerns such as unemployment, low education, poor relationships with the mother of their child(ren), and inadequate living conditions. These are critical issues facing young dads, and even older fathers as well. However, an important question fathers asked is; what is a man? They ask this question to understand their role, because most urban fathers are absent in their life. Therefore, the fathers ask a logical question prior to assuming responsibility for a child to understand his role as a man.

1. How would you define manhood or what is a man?

2. Did you have any examples of a man in your life?

   __Yes
   __No

   If you answered yes, please explain your response below. (if you engaged in any social, recreational, or other activities please include).

3. Is fatherhood & manhood similar in nature?

   ___Yes
   ___No

   Please explain your response below

4. If you were/are a father what role would/did you play? (i.e., cook food, pay bills, for the family, etc). If you are not a father, what role do you think you would play?

5. Who is an ideal father image of a father to you? (They could be television character, persons in the community, or otherwise?)

6. Who were the Promise Keepers and what was their motive for operating?

7. What was the cause or motivation for the Million Man March?

8. Do you think the Men's Movement of the Promise Keepers and the Million Man March was effective? Why or Why not? (Please explain below)

9. What was the women's movement about in the 60's?

10. Do you think the women's movement was successful?

11. How do you feel about feminism? (Please explain below)

THREE HOTS AND A COT

One day in my community-based organization, a young man engaged in a conversation with me. We talked about his challenges in obtaining employment. He stated everywhere he completed an application for a job, no one called him back for an interview because he had a criminal record. It so frustrated him seeking employment he was willing to commit another crime to return to prison. He justified it by saying, "At least I will have three hot square meals and a cot along with shelter." His overwhelming statement left me speechless. I was emotionally taken aback by his statement. But this statement reflected the reality of hundreds and thousands of African American and Latino men who have been incarcerated and who have mainstreamed back into the community.

"In 2008, one in one hundred American adults was behind bars. That's 2.3 million people. The United States imprisons more of its citizens than any other country in the world. American prisons offer a grim portrait of our country's underclass. One in thirty-six Hispanic adults is currently incarcerated, as is one in nine black men aged twenty to thirty-four. One in three black men will be imprisoned in his lifetime. Although illegal drug use is equally prevalent among white and black males, a black man is five times more likely to get arrested for it. A higher percentage of the black population is imprisoned in America than in South Africa at the height of apartheid. The proportion of young black men who are incarcerated has risen to the highest rate ever measured, said Allen J. Beck, the chief prison demographer for the Bureau of Justice Statistics, the statistical arm of the Justice Department." [30]

Our cities and communities are overloaded with young men and even women coming out of corrections. The prison system has become a revolving door. The notion that prison systems rehabilitate criminals has no significant evidence. But certainly we bare the truth it is a money-producing industry. Prisons over decades have become privatized. In 2008, the average cost to house a prisoner for one year in the United States was $23,876. In some states, like Rhode Island, "it costs $45,000, the same as a year's worth of tuition, room and board at Brown University." States like Connecticut spend "as much money on its prisons as it does on higher education. In twenty years, average state spending on corrections has nearly quintupled, to $49 billion. Although crime rates are dropping, this number continues to climb."[31]

The prison industries or industrial complexes conduct business with major corporations in the United States. Many prisons have become privatized, or they are allowed to contract services with companies. Some prisons are not exclusively under federal or state control or management. Any corporation or company in the free world or market can purchase prisons. Some say prison privatization serves as an investment opportunity. It is highly competitive. Millions and billions of dollars pass through the prison system. "From 1980 to 1994, while the number of federal and state prisoners increased by 221 percent, the number of inmates employed in prison industries jumped by 358 percent. Prison industries sales have skyrocketed during those years from $392 million to $1.31 billion. And they're not just making license plates."[32] Such companies as Trans World Airlines use prisoners to book flights. "Microsoft has used Washington State prisoners to pack and ship Windows software. AT&T has used prisoners for telemarketing; Honda, for manufacturing parts; and even Toys 'R' Us for cleaning and stocking shelves for the next day's customers."[33]

Prison privatization is no new fad in American society. For a hundred to two hundred years, privatization of prisons has existed. Private entrepreneurs have owned prisons for a profit. The state and federal governments contracted private owners to operate and manage a facility or to lease or contract labor to private companies. These prisons aimed to turn a profit for the state or at least pay for themselves. For instance, in the "mid-1800s state legislatures awarded contracts to operate Louisiana's first state prison, Auburn and Sing Sing penitentiaries, and others. These institutions became models for the entire sections of the nation where privatized prisons became the norm for the later century." (Covert Action Quarterly, fall 1993 issue Prisons for Profit, by Phil Smith)[34]

"In 1885, Texas forced mostly African American inmates to haul granite for building the new state capitol. These men, some of whom had been born into slavery, had become slaves once again. ... For most of the last century, prisoners were regularly leased out to plantation and factory owners. Guards whipped inmates for failing to meet quotas or for other work infractions."[35]

"In the 1950s, prison authorities, unions, and private companies reached a compromise on the issue of prison labor. The federal government and states agreed that prisoners should work as a means of rehabilitation. Inmate-produced goods would be used inside prisons or sold only to government agencies—and would not compete with private businesses or labor." Prison authorities, along with entrepreneurs, politicians, and private prison operations, are in the process of overturning that long held political consensus.[36]

In some states, more money is allocated to prisons than higher education. Prisons are known as growth industries. In 1994, "federal, state, and local governments spent an estimated $30 billion for their prison systems." In 1975, they only spent $4 billion.[37] In nearly two decades, the government spent seven times that amount for prisons. A significant portion of dollars was allocated for the construction of new facilities or prison complexes. In several states, prison construction has become commonplace. Prisons have become like fast-food chains, hotel conglomerates, or any other new corporations on the market.

The prison industry is one of the fastest-growing industries in the nation. "Corrections Corporation ranks among the top-five-performing companies on the New York Stock Exchange over the past three years. The value of its shares has soared from $50 million when it went public in 1986 to more than 3.5 billion."[38] Scores of Fortune 500 companies invest in the prison industry. Allstate, Merrill Lynch, Shearson Lehman, Goldman Sachs, and Prudential and other companies profit directly from the production, intensive labor, and involvement of the inmates.

While privatization of prisons continues to flourish on the backs of the socially and economically frail, politicians often set the tempo in determining who goes to jail. Policy decisions determine the number of people who are sent to prison. They receive political points by having a tough-on-crime policy that received notoriety during the Reagan era. With this policy in effect, the prison population soared through the 1980s, "making the U.S. the unquestioned world leader in jailing its own populace. By 1990, 421 Americans out of every 100,000 were behind bars, easily outdistancing our closest competitors, South Africa and the then USSR." By the 1990s the U.S. rate climbed to 455. In other words, the number of people jailed and in prison on any given day topped 1.2 million, up from fewer than 400,000 at the start of the Reagan era.[39]

The tough-on-crime policies appear to protect the public, but they are biased. Many politicians may express these policies reduce crime or create a safe and healthier community. And even more, they express the privatization of prisons saves or reduces tax spending because private owners manage the financial responsibilities of the prison. However, the cost of tough-on-crime policies extends beyond the reduction of tax dollars or spending. As a matter of fact, the amount of government dollars put toward prisons has not decreased. It has increased. Since the

1990s, the government has increased its spending six fold. Furthermore, the price of prison privatization filters beyond tax dollars and government spending. Privatization has little regard for human well-being and social development and rehabilitation. These policies seem to target poor Euro-Americans, blacks, Hispanics, Asians, and Native Americans. They usually lack training and marketable skills. Statistics reveal a disproportionate number of blacks, who comprise only 13 percent of the entire population and make up only 13 percent of those who use drugs regularly, make up 35 percent of the total number of people arrested for drug possession, 55 percent of those convicted for possession, and 74 percent of the entire number serving a possession sentence.[40]

Political decisions affect society overall. They influence the decisions and behaviors of the public. Whereas legislation could be devised in respect to privatized prisons, these institutions are viewed as solutions to the state and federal prison systems. Support emphasizes all the advantages or savings of public tax dollars. But it rarely discusses the underlying bottom line of profit gain in exchange for the human soul. It fails to acknowledge the recidivism rate of those who leave the private correctional systems and return because of a lack of skills and ability to survive in the ever-changing world.

> *Men respond to leadership in a most remarkable way and once you have won his heart, he will follow you anywhere.*
>
> —*Vince Lombardi*

Discussion Questions & Exercises

Vocabulary Words/Character Identification
Apartheid/South Africa
Prison privatization

Three Hots & A Cot

A young man stated after he completed numerous job applications, no one called him back for an interview because he had a criminal record. It was so frustrating seeking employment that he was willing to commit another crime and return to prison. He later stated, "At least I will have three hot square meals and a cot along with shelter.

1. As a society do you think we created this type of condition for those who've been incarcerated not to succeed?

    _____Yes
    _____No

    Explain your response below_____
    _____
    _____
    _____
    _____
    _____

2. Is going to jail for young African Americans males is like a badge of honor, or becoming a part of a social club or organization?

    _____Yes
    _____No

Explain your response below _____

_____

_____

_____

_____

_____

3. Why do you think the number of African Americans incarcerated is higher than other races; white, Latino, Asian, etc?

4. Can we as a society fix this problem of incarceration among youth and young adults?

   ____Yes
   ____No

   Explain your response below _____

   _____

   _____

   _____

   _____

   _____

5. Do you think our society discriminates against minorities (Black, Latino, immigrants, etc)?

   ____Yes
   ____No

Explain your response below_____

JEWELS AND THE CROWN

Each year in the month of January, the fatherhood or male program community-based organizations convene in the city of Newark to discuss strategies to help build momentum for Men's Health Month or Father's Day event for June. During several initial meetings, the group discussed various events and programs it desired to implement. The committee members were very enthusiastic about who they wanted to have as front-liners that year. One person in particular was the former governor Christie Whitman. She was a conservative leader who certainly believed in family values. The committee forwarded a formal letter to her office, requesting her participation as the keynote speaker at this fatherhood event for June 1995. The committee conducted numerous meetings in planning for the upcoming event. As the days progressed, no correspondence of her attending came from the governor's office. Certainly, she had hundreds of other residents in the state who requested her participation, so the community programs waited patiently.

As spring arrived, an urgent community bulletin notice went out to several organizations to attend a press conference regarding a statement by the governor of New Jersey. The community in Essex County was in an uproar because the governor had allegedly made a statement about fathers in Newark playing a game called *jewels in the crown*. The *New York Times*, in a March 1995 interview with a London publication, stated Ms. Whitman tried to underscore her view by recounting a story she heard from a young mother about black men who bragged about the babies they had fathered out of wedlock, calling them *jewels in the crown*.[41] The governor expressed black young men in Newark were involved with impregnating women for recreational pleasure. Those words ran through the core of the Newark community like a bitter chill to the bones.

At the press event, the governor's public comments incensed youths from a local high school and adults from the community. One young man on the podium stated it appalled him that the highest officer in the state would make such negative comments about African American young men. As the press conference continued, the press wanted to know about other programs in the city and state and the players nationally involved with this issue. The media also addressed the local assembly of politicians who coordinated the event, asking about the next steps. The officials stated the governor would not receive votes from the people of this country.

After the press event, the media aired an interview with one of the community leaders. This issue became a hot item in the state of New Jersey. As a community supporter and activist on issues related to fathers, I was interviewed by a number of radio stations, such as WCBS. The interviews began to focus not only on black fathers but also on race. The question became "Is this only a black issue, or do all communities and ethnic groups face young people getting pregnant?" As statistics demonstrated, this issue of teenage pregnancy and fathers behaving badly was not an issue only related to one ethnic group; groups' numbers of teenage pregnancies were significantly high during that period.

June approached. The committee finally heard from the governor's office. She was interested in attending the pre–Father's Day celebration. Through much coordination with the governor's office, they prepared for her committed attendance. On June 13, 1995, the governor agreed to participate in the celebration of fathers in the city of Newark at one of the local colleges. Every local media network was represented: the

CBS and NBC radio stations, the *Star-Ledger* and *New York Times* newspapers, and so on. They were in full array. She made a statement about fathers. It is as follows.[42]

> Whenever we talk about traditional welfare programs and social services, we tend to focus almost exclusively on the role and responsibility of the mother. Unfortunately, that approach cuts fathers out of the picture. And that's wrong. Children need the structure, the discipline, and added support that two parents are more likely to provide. In short, kids need their dads as well as their moms.
>
> So the question before us is, How can we balance the equation to keep moms and dads in their children's lives?
>
> We start by recognizing the importance of fathers to their children and by expecting all fathers to meet their parental obligations. However, when we talk about parental responsibility, we must bear in mind that many of these fathers have a lot of growing to do. They lack the skills a parent needs. They know little about child development and family planning. They face enormous social pressures. And their economic prospects are not bright.
>
> But we must recognize that most fathers really love their children and want to be there for them. Some of them just need a little help and guidance or just someone who will listen to them. We are here today to salute a program that for years has provided that help, guidance, and understanding for more than 1,000 young men. ... This community-based program really covers all the bases. It provides training and job placement. It offers GED classes, individual and family counseling, and health services. It furnishes legal aid and housing programs. It teaches parenting skills.

The state of New Jersey is very fortunate to have landmark programs that bring out the very best in young parents and find them the tools to improve their lives and the lives of their children. There were numerous media networking agencies present to discuss this important issue in the state of New Jersey, which had national interest and concerns as well. They had various comments about this event, such as the following:

Asbury Park Press: A young man said he could not believe young black males played a game called the *jewels and the crown* in which they compete to see who can father the most out-of-wedlock babies.

Home News Tribune: Many young fathers need help and guidance to grow up themselves while facing the responsibilities of raising their children.

When encountering these young men on a daily basis, you can learn tremendous lessons. As a community support advocate for many years, I've worked with thousands of young fathers and men in the community. I have discovered they have an amazing world, residing in the inner city. The urban lifestyle or inner-city community did, or does, include a fast-paced environment. For many of these young men, life is about survival, coping with the hustle and bustle of daily living, not just dealing with the baby-mama drama or child support or aid for their young but just simply managing their own lives and existence. On a daily basis, these young men would come to the office to talk about their issues, successes, or failures in being young men. Oftentimes, they dealt with lots of inner pain from growing up, whether it involved their relationship with their baby's mother or their getting arrested, having family-related matters or gang-related affairs, completing their education, obtaining employment, or other issues. They were really asking for help, needing someone to listen to them.

I discovered my role wasn't necessarily to fix their problems but to help them process and resolve the problems through their own volition or thought process. Oftentimes, they would just drop in. There have been times when their inaction has made them very emotional. It surprised me if a man would break down and cry because of his inner hurts and conflict, may be because he really desired to become a good father but his circumstances hindered his ability to move forward. Perhaps he was not employed, his baby's grandmother opposed his involvement, he did not know how to negotiate child support, and he simply did not know ways to handle difficult matters.

For instance, if a young man was unemployed, the mother at times would not allow him to see the child. This would extremely trouble him. Thus, the father needed someone who could advocate for and help him understand his legal rights and responsibilities. In this type of program, advocacy was extremely important. The young men needed to know what buttons to push in order for them to progress in society. In many cases, the father had experienced hardships. He saw systems such as child support as punitive networks. He felt guilty in most cases before the case stood before the judge. Because of these men's bad experiences and other horror stories told of child support enforcement demands, the system scared them.

Oftentimes, the father had every right to be afraid. The child support enforcement agency began a new campaign in New Jersey to ensure fathers paid child support through its system. The campaign targeted what are known as *deadbeat dads*, or fathers who owe back pay on child support or perhaps don't pay at all. In this campaign, child support decided to round up these fathers to collect child support. Occasionally, the agency could suspend some of the fathers' driver's licenses. The fathers felt the child support agency didn't have mercy on them. Child support had developed a special task force to raid the fathers' homes and detain them until they met the obligation or established payment plans.

The problem with many of these young men was actually layers of problems plagued them; child support was just one of many. If I were to give a brief overview of those who entered the office, it would be as follows.

- About 85–90 percent were unemployed.
- About 35–40 percent had not completed high school, either by dropping out or by still being in school.
- About 65 percent came from homes with single-female heads of households.
- About 35 percent had a juvenile or adult record.
- More than 50 percent were first-time fathers needing assistance, with an average age of seventeen to eighteen.

Each one of these qualities affected the others; for example, if a young man dropped out of high school, it became extremely difficult for him to obtain employment. Thus, he may have engaged in making fast money selling drugs. Then this led to incarceration, becoming a nonproductive citizen, or death. For most of these youngsters, the issue of economics was their driving force. Approximately 90 percent or more of these youngsters now attend the program on a volunteer basis. Usually, they attend out of the need to obtain employment. They need employment, for many of them have desperate situations.

One of the young fathers shared his account of the urgent matter of feeding his child. One day while sitting on the porch of his apartment, he needed to provide milk to his child. He was unemployed. He didn't have any income. So he contemplated robbing someone just so his child could have milk and shelter. He felt trapped in a dilemma of wanting to feed his child by his legal means or having to feed his child through illegal means. Fortunately, the community outreach program just so happened to contact the young man about some other issues, but he shared his need to feed his hungry child. The program was able to accommodate his needs and provide him with resources for his family.

The struggles of these young fathers and mothers are too many to mention and explore. But there is another side of the coin worth reflecting on. Certainly, our social programs are filled with horror stories of destitute families needing help to survive the daily trials of life. Families grasp for help by any means to continue, and oftentimes, the stories give a part of the account; the flip side of hope is seemingly dismissed. As a larger society, we exploit the most vulnerable in our community, especially our young urban males. The media, who often tell the story, may view a young man who is unemployed, uneducated, and unfamiliar with his legal rights. He gets brought before a larger society to reveal his story. Oftentimes, the story is biased. It doesn't provide an accurate assessment of the entire account of the individual. As some say, they want to sell the story.

Case in point, over the years, national media networks have portrayed Newark fathers and families for at least two decades. In their documentaries, they examine the lives of urban males or African Americans residing in the community. Most of the young men they have featured have had some type of social appendage or issue, such as an economic challenge, unemployment, minimal education, or perhaps just a high school diploma. The media would follow them for a year or more throughout the community. They would illustrate them as living in impoverished conditions and having dysfunctional families. The difficulty with these documentaries and similar ones was they never revealed the issues of other ethnic groups and the disparities existing in other communities. The numbers many of the documentaries demonstrated could not demonstrate true significance and show true validity. In addition, when some of the major media networks conducted documentaries, they never reported many of the social community programs or the success stories of these young men.

Reliable sources have stated that prior to releasing the stories, they left the organizations of change on the editing floor. In other words, they modified the original idea they proposed to these organizations that they would focus on. Usually, they ended up focusing on sensationalizing the stories for ratings. It certainly became deceptive broadcasting. Moreover, the media often provided and continue to provide a limited perspective of the matter and do not show the broader view. The media leave the viewing audience thinking fatherlessness is only an African American problem, but in reality, the numbers of fathers among all ethnic groups continue to decrease. Perhaps the numbers of African Americans seem at a faster decline, but in every category, the number of fatherless cases erodes the American family structure. The portrayal of fathers or men in our society continues to diminish. The '50s, *father knows best* generation was somewhat the theme of our society. The father was like the president of a company; the mother was like the CEO. But as time continued to the '90s, songs like "My Baby Daddy" became the theme of our modern day. The roles of fathers have minimized.

Nevertheless, scores of fathers who attended the community-based program have had great success, which wasn't always broadcasted. Some of the young men became detectives, police officers, entrepreneurs, ministers, community activists, and realtors. During many individual and group sessions, the fathers grew by leaps and bounds. We experienced a sort of outpouring, infusing and transforming men's lives. Young men who didn't know the direction or path to take for their career, business, education, or employment discovered it. The community-based program was inspirited, causing men and families to experience a transformation of sorts socially, emotionally, and economically. Every facet of the community-based program empowered participants to accomplish their goals or maintain a sense of health and well-being. The next several accounts illustrate the program's invigoration and inspiration.

A young man was scheduled for court on a particular day because of a substance abuse charge or for selling illegal substances in the community. This young man had enrolled in the program for support. He seemed committed to his child. He always had his child when he came to this agency. He informed the staff of his court date and discussed the charges. As a result of him going to court, the program began to rally support letters and advocate on his behalf. Several community-based organizations joined in support with support letters to aid him. All the social services partners seemed fond of him. They thought he was genuine and he possibly had a good future ahead of him.

The morning came. One of the staff attended court with the young father. The staff hoped for good news that day. We were all optimistic. So the proceedings began, after two men came before the judge. The young man came to the bench. The judge read his charges and told him to prepare to go to jail that day and to take a seat and wait for that sentence. Our hearts went through the floor. We thought we could do nothing, especially when the judge gave his command.

As the young father went to his seat, waiting for his sentencing, the public defendant went to speak with him in the back of the room. As they went, one of the staff went with them. When seated before the public defendant, he stated, "The judge is spitting fire. Everyone in the courtroom today is seemingly going to jail." Earlier, as the staff sat in court, the judge had sent African American men to jail one by one. So the public defendant said, "That's the story."

The young man replied, "What about my son?"

The public defendant responded, "The Division of Youth and Family Services will take him away and bring him into the foster care system." Then, the public defendant inquired to the staff person. The staff person replied we had letters of support for this young man.

As we went back into the courtroom and before the judge, he asked who we were. The staff person stated his interest in being there for the young man. The judge asked, "Why do you think he would be good for the program?" We stated that he was consistent and appeared very fond of his child.

Then, the prosecutor stood up, stating, "The young father violated the statutes of the state of New Jersey and its citizens."

Finally, the judge gave a verdict. He stated, "Fathers are important. Children need their fathers. Therefore, the court is placing him on probation, under the guidance of the community-based program." Sounds of unbelief arose in court after the verdict because the judge changed his own decree from earlier in the day. The verdict favored young fathers; the young man went home a free man.

A second account concerns another young man who needed support from the program. At the end of a year, in December, I received a phone call about a young man needing support. He was a patient in a local hospital. He wanted to come in and talk about the program and his near-death experience. My community-based organization gave an audience to him. He began to tell us a horrific story, saying several young men in the community abducted him. He stated he was falsely accused of harming someone's family member. He utterly denied the rumors or charges from these men. But these men overpowered him and drove him to an isolated area on the outskirts of the city. Not knowing what would happen to him, he felt fear grip his being.

The men blindfolded him and tied his hands. He didn't know what they would do next. They pulled him out of the car they put him in and paraded around him, reminding him of what he had done, and all of a sudden, they began to shoot him. The bullets riddled his body. The impact of the bullets forced him to fall to the grand. In his heart, he said, *I'm not going to die … I'm not going to die.* As the abductors left the scene, leaving him for dead, he began to walk until he collapsed. Someone saw him and called the police and later rushed him to the hospital. As he lay in the hospital for several weeks, he was informed about our community-based program. And when he left the hospital, he wanted to enroll in our agency. So he was elated.

He stated he always wanted to be part of this agency because, and he showed all the bullet marks on his body. Then, he stated, "Can you help me live just like other men that have come to your program?" He asked, "What does your program do to help men live?" I began to pray with him and provided emotional support for him to cope with this traumatic situation. For several weeks, I stayed in touch with him. I wrote a support letter for him to obtain employment at a construction company, along with counseling and spiritual guidance. But then I did not see him for several years.

One day, as I walked down the corridors of my agency, this young, familiar-looking man walked in my direction. I didn't recognize him. But he recognized me. He asked me if I remembered him. I stated, "Not really."

He stated, "You gave me support and prayed with me. And today, I am free, and my life is fulfilled. I came by to say thank you. You helped me greatly. Thank you." He walked away as a messenger sent from above. Sometimes, the thank-yous are few and far between.

The third account relates to the annual events our agency conducts in the community for homeless families. Every year, our community-based program provides a pre-Thanksgiving holiday dinner for the fathers and homeless families in the community. It is our premiere event of the year. We have a world of wonderful dishes, like turkey, chicken, macaroni and cheese, spaghetti, green beans, and desserts like cake, pie, and everything else. It is actually a feast. We may serve twenty-five to fifty families. Many of the fathers help serve the meal. During mealtime, we have speakers, entertainment, and lots of laughter and fun. Because of the nature of the occasion, many homeless families look toward moving on in their lives, such as getting an apartment or a job or going back to school. At the event, we allow them the opportunity to give testimonies of their aims or desires in moving forward. After all the entertainment and guest speakers, the families have a moment to share their hearts' desires. These parents, especially mothers, express their ambitions in raising their children in their own dwelling place or home. Many of the participants may share tears of pain, yet gratitude for the program embracing them and providing them with support.

At the end of one of these Thanksgiving feasts and celebrations, we heard numerous testimonies of many of the mothers' goals and aims to move forward. But on that particular day, a young mother walked up to me during our closing song, "Reach Out and Touch (Somebody's Hand)," as the families sang while I played the saxophone. She interrupted me as I played. I became self-conscious of why she interrupted me while I played my instrument. She began to share a story about staying in the homeless shelter. Tears began to go down her face. The welfare office had sent her to the shelter because she was homeless due to a broken relationship. She had been involved with a young man and had a child by him. She deeply loved him. But as time went on, he no longer wanted to be involved with her. The emotional pain of no longer sharing love as they had and her reliance upon him overwhelmed her. Her heart was broken seemingly into a thousand or more pieces. She couldn't cope with the emotional agony and trauma of the breakup. As a result, she cut her wrist in an attempt to commit suicide.

She was hospitalized for a period of time, certainly feeling the agony and pain of her lost love. The hospital then placed her in a homeless shelter along with her beautiful two-year-old daughter. She had recently been placed in the shelter because she didn't have anywhere to stay. Several hours after the hospital released her, the entire shelter was invited to this event. Unknowingly, she sat and dined with us. She then poured her heart out about her traumatic experience. But the story didn't end at the misfortune of her love life, of not being loved.

She began to talk about this event as her moment of inspiration. She stated when she came into the room for the event, she didn't know what this program did. She thought her inner pain was insurmountable. But as she participated, it renewed her hope. She stated, "When I came in the room for the event, I had the hospital band around my arm, feeling vulnerable and afflicted by the pain of my lost love." But as she expressed herself, something happened; she tore off the hospital band on her arm and threw it in the garbage because she now believed she could make it. What a moment. We began to cry together and embrace. She now felt inspired and empowered to live.

Each year, the program witnesses men and women receiving new strength and renewed hope with a surge of power to live productive lives. Throughout the community-based program's history, men and women have obtained new leases on life. Many accounts exist of young men assuming leadership roles in both their families and the community. These young men are the leaders of today and are involved in transforming the lives of other young men and women in society. Certainly, numerous accounts exist of young men who arose from beneath the rubble of despair and misfortune, from the emotional torment of lost love, from the social grip and trap of hustling and dealing to make fast money in street life, and from the death wounds inflicted by violent men.

Through years of abuse and devastation, many African American men have come through generations of racism and social neglect, poverty, war, imprisonment, injustice, victimization, inhumane treatment, isolation, and brutality. This community-based organization designed a vehicle through which it serviced the needs of men and families in the community. This agency constructed a framework for young men and their significant others and family members to achieve success. These ideas and constructs have their roots in community collaboration and partnerships. Each entity of the community must engage with society, education, business, faith-based groups, the armed forces, and housing. Every organization and corporation must contribute to the greater function of the community. We must make a concerted effort as a community to partner up and bring about change. We produce the engine to create this synergy through the spirits of those individuals of belief and faith who lend themselves to a unified approach, not politically motivated but for the human wealth of mankind. It's driven through individuals whose passion speaks with a voice not for material wealth but for the welfare of the souls of men.

Discussion Questions & Exercises

Vocabulary Words/Character Identification
Allegedly
Vulnerable
Contemplated
Deadbeat dads
Punitive
Abducted
Victimization

JEWELS AND THE CROWN

Former New Jersey Governor Christie Todd Whitman once made a controversial remark in a British publication stating that black teenage fathers played a game called "Jewels in the Crown" when they fathered children out of wedlock. Whitman, who received criticism over her comments, also was accused of playing into racial stereotypes of black teenage fathers. At the time, black unwed mothers were used to illustrate how young black males were having children to score points and street credibility among their peers.

Discussion questions

1. Do you think teens engage in sex only for recognition and social acceptance?

    ____Yes ____No ____Other reason (please explain)

2. Do you feel sex should be recreational without responsibility of it?

3. How do your peers see engaging in sex;

   a. _____A serious relationship
   b. _____Recreational Activity
   c. _____Both
   d. _____Other (explain)_____

4. What are some of the challenges of engaging in sex as a teen?

5. If you were a parent that had children in middle and High School, what would you tell them about sex?

6. Do you think boys are only interested in having sex?

7. Do you think girls play games in relationships to manipulate boys to get involved or not to get involved?

TOOLS AND APPROACHES TO EMPOWER MEN, FAMILIES, AND COMMUNITIES

We as a society grapple with not knowing how to address the social dilemmas of incarceration, high school dropout rates, gang violence, school (non-gang-related) violence, and community teenage pregnancy rates and health disparities. Such news of despair often overwhelms and frustrates us. It infiltrates our living rooms through the disturbing news of our family members who indulge in riotous or careless living. The message of hope seems to whisper as near silence as corruption, crime, and immorality roar relentlessly, rendering trepidation and fear upon men's souls. In such a manner, the masses wonder of the vitality of the present and future of their communities. Many question the significance of our political, economic, and educational systems.

With the trials of past years of discrimination and humiliation, and our present bouts of social deterioration, it often leaves communities to minimize vital tomorrows or the dreams of great men like Dr. King, whose vision diminished before us. But we must not succumb to the negative elements that try to consume us. We must become tenacious in transforming our world from the inside out. We must see the human design as a perpetual well of resources and opportunities for a productive citizenry, reliant upon neighborly coexistence or unifying souls of purpose to enhance the human race, connecting them to faith and hope and supporting men and families in their journey to their own unique place in the universe.

Over the years, I and a host of wonderful community leaders have assisted men in identifying their own strength and potential. Through my divine creator's help, we have humbly attempted to understand and develop programs to aid young men in becoming responsible men, good fathers, and leaders. As a community advocate and organizer, I fortunately have some approaches and tools that have aided me in enhancing young men in the community, and I have a collaborative team of individuals and family members that has been instrumental in achieving viable support for young men and families. The following information outlines and demonstrates our views and success. I've illustrated the model utilized in this construct for producing a viable organization for young men and families.

In today's society, employment or having financial resources is extremely vital to young men. I believe money is attached to men's ego and pride. Many times, I hear young men say, "I feel better about myself when I have money in my pocket." These young men have a lot of pride. They desire the American dream, even though some of them try to obtain it in an illegal fashion. Many of them don't desire to get involved in selling illegal substances, but economically, it appears to be easy money, and it doesn't require attending school. It doesn't have the requirements of working every day, punching the clock, and making wages. But the majority of the young men involved in this social program are just motivated by getting a job. They want to do better for themselves, but they sometimes face great obstacles.

The news of them becoming a father is important to them but can also add more pressure. Oftentimes, people ask, "Why do young men deny or run away from their responsibilities and not man up to them?" The answer does not apply for every father but for many of the men our organization has encountered. One reason fathers may not assume their role as fathers can be viewed in the lack of maturity they have developed to raise a child. Most of these young men didn't plan to become fathers. They say, "It sort of happens," in their life. They enjoy having the sex but do not want the responsibility that follows. Mentally, they don't try to figure out or process the duties and everything attached to raising a child. They think of the pleasure of the relationship.

I have experienced sixteen-year-old men coming to the office to learn about pregnancy and having a child. But they do not return until two to three years later, then stating they now feel ready for the relationship, because they couldn't provide emotionally, mentally, economically, or socially before. The true problem mounts onto fatherhood for them when they realize the mother will move on to another relationship. The child will perhaps or more likely call the new man his father. So many of them are not mature enough to have long-term healthy relationships. Many of them are still developing their own identities and experimenting with their adolescence, adding to all the messages they receive as youths. It is like a battlefield, trying to maneuver through to the other side of adolescence. One songwriter says of fathers in his lyrics, "That's just my baby daddy." His status as a father gets minimized to only being the baby's daddy—nothing else. He doesn't help nurture his child as the role model and man the child needs.

Thus, the economic factor motivates a father's participation in his child's life, but the reason he attends the program is also attached to an inner fear of not knowing what to do when the child is born. He may have layers of concern beneath his tough demeanor. Foremost, for fathers who haven't had fathers in their lives, they want to know what it means to be a man and a father, because it confuses them. They often ask what it means to be a man. Then we gradually get to answering what it means to be a father. Because of his lack of understanding about raising a child, he asks the program to answer this question. And certainly, because of his own father's absence in his life, he wants to be there for his child. He wants to compensate for the lack of support he had in his own development.

Many fathers express if their father was there, he would be farther up the road. He interprets fatherhood as acting as a breadwinner and having the economic wherewithal to become the head of the house, but beneath the surface of his being sometimes lay fear, uncertainty, confusion, hurt, and rejection. He may desire to be there for his child, but the issues he faces may overwhelm him; thus, he may feel better off not being there for the child.

Parenting Skills Education

Many fathers and also mothers need training to raise their children. This is an essential ingredient for fathers to aid in their children's development, but they do not always make education their priority. A significant number of young men are still very traditional in nature. They want to become the breadwinners. In the community-based organization, fathers would volunteer to come to the program 80–90 percent of the time, when compared to other young men who attended. Their driving motive for attending the program wasn't to obtain parenting skills as much as to obtain employment. Many of them articulated this is important, but the most significant part of being a father is feeding the family. They could learn how to feed, diaper, and develop healthy relationships with their children to meet their basic needs. Oftentimes, our office would receive calls from the courts, family services, the Division of Youth and Family Services, the Office of Juvenile Justice, and other agencies for parenting training. Fathers and mothers would attend these services for several weeks. Then our organization would forward a letter to the appropriate agency, indicating the participant attended.

Community Outreach

I find working with young men and their families a tremendous experience. It is a wonderful blessing. I have learned the greatest approach for engaging fathers or males or even people in general is to meet people where they are or find a neutral place. Too often, we want to bring participants and people to our organizations or activity. We must first be willing to meet people on neutral ground. We must engage them in their particular place. This doesn't necessarily mean we have to meet them in their home. Understanding their point of view is essential. Many of our greatest encounters in recruiting young men happen at events or activities outside our workplace where males congregate, such as at barbershops, sporting events, and special social functions. The rationale behind this is you afford the individual comfort in meeting him in neutral territory. It allows the young man to feel more relaxed and that you share a common interest, perhaps going to an athletic competition, a shared barbershop, a golf course, or a basketball court. The true goal to this endeavor is to develop relationships, not to take anything away from the individual mission of the organization. You want to connect with the individual and to later address his needs. The greater mission in social service is to empower the individual, assisting him in the overall development.

I have met individuals who desperately needed support. They faced life-and-death situations. In the social services field, this is almost commonplace. But I will recount a specific situation, during our outreach mission in the community. We were providing health screenings. We aimed to identify men and women who did not have medical insurance. Even though we targeted men, we included women too. As you know, women are prone to access doctors more frequently than men. However, while we were out in the community, a fairly healthy-looking woman came to our health station from the streets to obtain a blood pressure screening. I engaged her in a conversation about her health and encouraged her to get a screening. She stated she had not frequented a doctor for health examinations in years. So she agreed to the screening. While we screened her, the nursing staff discovered she had almost had a crisis. Her blood pressure was so elevated that she was on the verge of collapsing on the street. The staff immediately dispatched all to call for an ambulance. It arrived in minutes and took her to the hospital.

Incidents of this nature may not always occur while doing health screenings in the field, but similar social crises may occur. Scores of young men and women may contemplate suicide and need housing. Certainly, you are not everything to all people, but you become a resource and a conduit for someone else to live. The reality is not everyone wants help; sometimes, people may get stuck and refuse your aid, but as people servicing in social, religious, or nursing positions or similar roles, we must offer support not out of obligation but out of compassion. I think the key in working in the community or any other field is knowing your limitations. Establish your support network and your boundaries so that you may be effective in the field. You serve as a soldier when conducting community outreach. One must be equipped with the necessary resources to safeguard the individual and the community you serve to bring health. And by the way, don't try to save the world. Take incremental steps in aiding persons one person at a time. You can easily burn out.

Social and Community Networking

I recall when I was a child, my mother at times told my brothers and sisters to go next door to the neighbors' house and get some butter to make pancakes or biscuits. She had the flour, milk, and eggs, but somehow or another, she didn't have the other ingredients to make bread. Without any of these ingredients, bread would not have tasted delightful. And certainly, you wouldn't have wanted her to cook for you anymore, unless she got some lessons.

In a similar manner, effective communities need to have the ingredients that make up the whole. They link and unify resources to assist in establishing the whole. One should not be so concerned about whose names to mention but focus on assisting an individual in his development. Certainly, everyone wants to receive his portion of involvement, but we must begin to function as a whole entity. Many of our organizations function in a vacuum. Our organization puts its brand name on the product that it services. It puts it in lights, but only for the organization's recognition or glory. Our organizations at times become a greater focus of our operations than the customers we service. We spend more money on the construction of our organization than the health and well-being of the clients we service. Many of our institutions burden the customers with the costs for an increase in salary and other monetary gains.

Nevertheless, linking and unifying resources to assist in establishing the whole is imperative. Because of budget cuts and reduced staffing to operate social service businesses, it becomes imperative to collaborate or to develop partnerships. We need new approaches, such as working with corporations that share our vision or mission. We must operate social services as a corporation, treating individuals as customers with utmost care. For community agencies to survive in this economic crisis, we must be interconnected. Developing partnerships with other institutions assists us in connecting to the broader community. It allows us to service our young men in a greater capacity. We can track our customers through collective resources, which may give us a broader scope of the customers' needs, because oftentimes, the customers learn to operate from one social service to the next. Therefore, we must develop partnerships to help fathers and men facilitate the system.

Faith-Based Community

The faith-based community, especially in the African American community, has served as the main artery of our society's functioning. As previously illustrated, the faith community has been instrumental in every major occurrence or transition in American history from the Emancipation Proclamation in 1863 to the civil rights movement in the 1960s. The faith community has always been vocal on human rights issues. It has served as the moral conscience of America. Even today, the faith community still maintains her status in the community. Perhaps society in a larger purview may not accept its position on particular issues, but it has respectability in the overall community. In major social tragedies, the faith community unites to bring healing to situations or problems. Even where violence or other devastation occurs, the faith community has been a pillar in our society.

The faith community can continue its mission in bringing about social reform and strength for congregations and their neighbors. In recent years, much of our society has relied on government subsidies to support health and social initiatives and programs. Throughout many years and the many presidential and state government administrations, the government has been supportive and very generous in helping needy families and in establishing programs to aid those who seem misfortunate. It recalls the Clinton administration that introduced the faith-based initiatives that provided aid to innovative projects. These projects were or are housed in the faith community to continue efforts in strengthening youths and families.

Over the years, we have witnessed those dollars diminish. These dollars we once had to engage communities have significantly reduced or no longer exist. Therefore, the faith community has an awesome task of addressing the social needs of the community as it always has done, but now in a greater capacity. First, the church or faith community role today will compensate for the lack of governmental resources. Second, the faith community will need to develop networks with other entities in the community, such as businesses, the health field, education, and housing projects. Third, the faith community that's on the cutting edge addresses the holistic concerns of the people in both their congregation and community, including their social, spiritual, economic, educational, and health needs. Perhaps faith-based organizations may not have comprehensive services, but they have resources and connections to community resources. A biblical account states, "I wish above all things that you may prosper and be in health, even as your soul prospers" (3 John 1:2 AKJV). The interpretation is that the creator is not just interested in spiritually empowering individuals but in empowering every facet of their lives.

The faith community can participate in numerous collaborations or partnerships. It can adopt a school, mentorship activities, tutorial services, community health fairs, parent support groups, soup kitchens, and clothing and dress for success initiatives. Faith-based communities have to play a greater role now. People of today face new issues and problems.

The faith community can get more involved in numerous issues or social concerns. For instance, thousands of young men who are released from corrections or prison need resources to help them mainstream back into society. Perhaps your faith community may not necessarily establish a program, but it will provide resources and information to young men about reentry programs. The key to these initiatives is innovation that addresses the needs of the population one serves.

School-Based Initiatives or Parents

School-based initiatives are also vital to community enhancement. Most African American young men and women reside in absentee-father homes. Many youths and children lack positive adult male and sometimes female role models. People who could provide support in the emotional and social development of youths are absent or not available to assist.

For many years, my twin brother, Carl, and I have worked in elementary schools to help young people develop social skills, addressing issues like sexuality, teen pregnancy, dating, gang violence, peer pressure, bullying, relationships, and decision making and a series of trainings that focuses on youth development. First, schools should implement these efforts or similar programs throughout the school year. Conducting presentations or workshops on a one-time basis for youths, especially in urban communities, doesn't provide cohesiveness or fortitude to assist in impacting behavioral changes or modifications. Young people need continual reinforcement. Conducting small, manageable groups is important, perhaps fewer than fifteen or twenty youths or sometimes smaller groups. You will more likely reduce distractions with smaller numbers. You can provide information to larger audiences of youths, but the smaller groups help some young people become more attentive. Although some speakers are gifted and can command attention to help youngsters learn, most youths get distracted.

Second, it is important to develop specific goals for youths and allow students to participate in establishing the goals as well. Allow students to engage in the process of goal development. Sometimes, adults have a tendency to impose their views and say what they think and young people feel. Oftentimes, we misinterpret their needs until we ask them to be a part of the planning process or develop a clear path to their future.

Third, parental involvement in their children's education also has significance. Parents need to be involved in both their male and female youngsters' education process. Parents must set up boundaries to assist their children in their social, emotional, and intellectual development. For instance, they should have students establish homework time, do chores around the house, and engage in social activities with peers. Parents must set time limits and a schedule for the children to function. Parents must monitor their children's time, such as the amount of time they spend watching television, talking on the phone, and playing sports. Parents must stay engaged in their children's lives, especially during the formative elementary years. Oftentimes, children are left alone without appropriate supervision. Sometimes, parents have the responsibilities of work and other duties they need to perform; by the end of the day, they may feel too tired or need personal time. This can be very dangerous. Some children could have too much room or idle time, during which they can become vulnerable. Other children can come to the house for recreation and get into mischief, whether with sex or drugs. One writer once stated, "A child left to himself will bring the parent to shame." He or she must have limitations.

Today, we have scores of parents who are a shame because we, as their parents, didn't provide the structure for the children as they grew up. Parents must invest time in giving children guidance and support. One of the greatest challenges for most single mothers is raising children, especially the male child. It is true that children learn from modeling, not from the notion that many women say: "I am the man and woman too!" In our society, we experience many of our women playing extensive roles, because of the lack of fathers in the home. Motherhood most often overwhelms them, especially if they have more than one child to support. A mother provides food, clothes, and shelter and becomes involved in the children's affairs, perhaps doing two to three jobs to survive, then trying to maintain her sanity.

The situation of raising children today is unlike yesteryear; it can be trying to parents. It was a challenge even in disciplining the male child in my house. I recall my parents spanking me and my brother. They said, "You better not cry." Now, I want to say, man, it hurt. But because I wanted to be a man, I didn't cry, unless I couldn't bare it any longer. This type of language and behavior can damage kids. Over the years, I heard that boys or men shouldn't cry. I believe this to be one of the most damaging messages children or men can ever receive. These messages, sometimes sheared into the souls of young men, cause them to repress their emotions and their pain. Over time, the pain will likely intensify and cause males difficulty in relationships, on jobs, in families, with relatives, and so on.

In my role as a counselor, I have seen many angry young men who do not know how to express their emotions. They repress themselves for a long period of time until they are angry, not really knowing how to express emotion. They are angry because they feel neglected, their father abandoned them, they lack finances, or they live in poverty. They are incarcerated, lacking love and support. Thus, many of our school-aged youths bottle up hurts and pains without asking for help and sometimes not knowing how to ask. I recall my mother saying when I grew older, "I wanted to leave you all in the park," because having eight children was difficult without our father living with us.

Perhaps the question may be "What was or is the formula for a possible solution in rearing children? What did they do as parents that seemed to work in their time?" While discussing my mother's role and the roles of many parents of yesteryear, I found they had a four-step plan for their children.

1. They engaged in structured family activities. The brothers and sisters got involved with recreational activities, playing musical instruments, attending the library, or playing sports or other positive activities.

2. Neighbors, who were the people in the community parents deemed trustworthy, made sure things stayed intact if your mother or father wasn't home. They played a role as almost a second parent. If one of the children got into trouble in the community, a neighbor was allowed to spank or reprimand you. But then neighbors would also tell your parents about your misbehavior. The parents would then reprimand you as well or render *applied psychology* (in other words, whip ya).

3. Mentorship was another important ingredient. When my family went to church, we found it fun although it was structured and supportive. We participated in sports and cultural and recreational activities, met new friends, and enjoyed our youth. We had mentors there. Men in the church taught us music, arts, and culture and served in leadership capacities. And on a monthly basis, my brother Carl and I would visit the pastor with my mother. That frightened us because he wanted to make sure we did our best at all times. He would even say, "I want to see your report card." If we hadn't completed our assignment or we acted out, we were seemingly put in a den of lions, because we knew he would deal with the problem in a way we didn't want him to. He was certainly the village leader who helped hundreds upon hundreds of single mothers raise their children.

4. Spirituality was important in our family. It provided us with a kind of belief structure that told us everything would be all right. It helped us have faith in God. Certainly, black people couldn't have faith in the system because of racism and discrimination, but we had faith to believe and trust in God. It gave our family a foundation that if everything around us seemed to

get destroyed, we knew a greater power in the universe would guide and protect us. We believed even when someone set our apartment in the projects on fire while we attended church. In our discomfort and grief, we had hope. We believed we would go to a better place. We didn't know how, but we had faith. And I tell you, we did; we moved to another city with better housing conditions. From the multidwelling apartment in the projects, we moved to a house in East Orange, New Jersey. We had faith in God. This was passed down from generation to generation. It was the foundation of our existence.

One great man stated how we should raise children. He stated with "roots and wings." When one leaves the nest, he must be able to take the roots of his heritage and his family with him so he can continue the generation and the legacy.

Political Networking

Occasionally, it is important to engage your city, local, or state officials in addressing issues related to your organization. Government officials are the ones to ideally fight for your organization and the people of the community. We must hold them accountable to their word and leadership. You must have confidence they deem your issue important. You need to establish relationships with your community leaders. They need to see you at community functions, or you can invite them to your events that speak to specific situations or problems in the city and community. They should be a link or resource to greater funding opportunities to assist in your organization's functioning. They should be the ones to advocate for you in the state office.

Bishop David Barns (black suit and hat) and community leaders campaigning on the steps of city Hall, Newark, NJ

In holding them accountable, you may have to write a letter or email to them about your agency and your mission. At times, you may have to become aggressive and conduct campaigns in the community on the steps of city hall or somewhere else with public visibility. Your passion must be evident for others to hear. For instance, if we need to get more men involved in frequently going to medical examinations, we engage with city officials, the faith-based community, schools, and the business community. We may host press conferences with mayors or other governing bodies about this critical issue and create a plan to impact the community, utilizing a top-down approach to address the issue.

The mission of the agency and organization is to bring the issue to the forefront of the community. As one of my community partners, Mr. Emmanuel Ruranga stated, "If a lion comes into the village, one must go to the highest part of the village or the hill to yell, 'A lion is in the village!' to alarm the people." Likewise, we must alert the village of the predator in our community. In other words, we must sound the alarm of dangers in our community from every point of being. Every person in leadership plays a significant role in breaking the cycle of despair, eliminating the social, economic, and health disparities in our community.

Business Community

Historically, the social community has functioned independently from the business community. Many social services have relied on government grants and contracts from the state and other federal or governmental entities. In the past, agencies functioned on government support and funding, programs survived year by year on government allocations. Organizations competed with other social service organizations to receive grant funding. This was the norm among our brothers and sisters in the social service arena. However, the government has since reduced or eliminated many of the social services once offered. It has completely knocked agencies off their feet or functioning.

Wherefore, community-based organizations need new approaches in servicing the community. The business community has to sit at the table to discuss the significance of its support. It is important to develop long-term and short-term strategies that will assist in strengthening communities and families. For instance, individuals may discuss investing in education for young males or youths. An agency may develop GED tutorials and mentorship programs to specifically address the educational needs of the population. The goal will be to examine the number of individuals obtaining a high school diploma or a GED or attending college to validate the programs' significance.

Your organization can also allow corporations to frequently interact with it to conduct workshops, job fairs, and financial management and entrepreneurial development training. Young men seek opportunities beyond selling drugs on the streets. As a community, we must provide young men with resources to empower them. Oftentimes, we misinterpret them and say pursuing their dreams and career ambitions does not interest them, but it does. We detach ourselves from them because of their past, sometimes criminal record. Our society is prone to disregard their talents and skills and even their appearance. We put down a barrier and won't allow them the opportunities to succeed.

Many young men come out of corrections with minor offenses or sometimes major offenses and seek a new life. Many of our corporate policies shut the door on possibilities for them, but we must create ways—checks and balances—that will help our society effectively screen them but willingly give them opportunities. We must rethink many of our institutional policies. Not everyone coming out of corrections wants better for him- or herself, but thousands do. But if we don't open the door of opportunity, then we all likewise perish because they want to survive, as all of us do.

> *That best portion of a good man's life, his little, nameless, unremembered acts of kindness and love.*
>
> —*William Wordsworth*

Discussion Questions & Exercises

Vocabulary Words/Character Identification
Social Dilemmas
Trepidation
Infiltrates
Mentorship

Tools and Approaches to Empower Men, Families, and Communities

I. The issues we dealt with 3-5 years ago is similar and yet different to today's challenges. Thus, I would like to brain storm and identify some of the most pressing issues and to develop strategies in addressing these problems.

Please list and identify the specific problems among men and families below. (Convene in a group for a discussion)

Identified Issues/problems

1.

2.

3.

4.

5.

6.

7.

II. As you convene in a group discuss 3 ways or recommendations to address the issues.

1a. Problem Area/Topic_____

b. Recommendations_____

_____
_____
_____
_____
_____

2a. Problem Area/Topic_____

b. Recommendations_____

_____
_____
_____
_____
_____

3a. Problem Area/Topic_____

b. Recommendations_____

_____
_____
_____
_____
_____

III. What are some first steps you can do to implement one or two of your recommendations?

(Example: Problem Area: To decrease youth gang violence- Forward a letter to the police department to arrange a meeting with sergeant or captain…)

1.

2.

3.

IV. What one or two things you can do to propel this issue forward and to engage the greater community involvement?

V. Is there a major person, stakeholder, community leader or organization that can help propel your mission or cause?

COMMUNITY ALLIANCES OR PARTNERSHIPS

In our community, many describe the inner city as having insurmountable problems. They say it is out of control and lacks support systems and alliances for networking to bring about a healthier community. We understand that we must break the cycle of broken communities and families, unraveling the pain of brokenness and generational despair. We must develop communities through collaboration and cooperation with partners from multiple disciplines or vast networks and partnerships.

For many years, we have developed a community network through engaging organizations, businesses, faith-based groups, education institutions, and so on and convened on a monthly basis to discuss strategies to impact specific concerns and issues of young men and families. The group or community focused on specific issues such as fatherhood and male issues. Over the years, a network or consortium of organizations has evolved into a community network addressing the needs of men. This consortium of program directors, coordinators, community leaders, educators, businessmen, and health professionals who work with males has worked on projects together to address many problems in the urban community. The consortium has convened to address a myriad of issues related to black males, especially due to the tremendous crisis in our neighborhoods.

The group of professionals has created numerous recommendations to assist communities in developing stronger and better neighborhoods. They are as follows.

- Learn how to envision or utilize young black males as a valuable resource.
- Share information and apply the different resources available to the right type of individual.
- Access and support community resources.
- Develop more sites for GED testing.
- Develop employment opportunities.
- Increase recreational activities.
- Enrich mentoring programs.
- Close generational gaps in the community in a cross-generational major effort.
- Unearth a resource guide on barbershops, mechanics shops, bodegas, and beauty salons available to the kids on the street.

In addressing fathers' needs, I've identified three major areas of need: health issues, education issues, and parenting issues.

Health Issues

Good health leads to the ability to work and get involved with the family. How should we address this issue of health information dissemination in the community? Provide information and resources for young men, especially the uninsured, to have better access to health care. Conduct male health fairs in your area. We hold them in community centers and community colleges, and we held our innovative one in barbershops. Identify a barber who will willingly give up his shop after hours to introduce health education activities. Conduct health screenings; for example, host screenings with incentives, such as tickets to a professional basketball or football event. And engage the media, such as local radio stations that young people listen to, in any health education efforts.

Education Issues

Increasing productivity and enhancing self-esteem through education improve decision making and worldview changes. You do better when you know better, but how do we do this? We believe that we should encourage more men to go into the field of early childhood education, both in elementary schools and day care centers. Fathers' involvement in schools will improve education. Fathers need to get involved in the PTA, afterschool programs, and chaperoning. We need to look at issues of financial aid, Upward Bound, and getting people to compete academically. We need to establish information centers targeted at fathers. Women have lots of information centers around; women can always find a way to get information, but men may not.

Parenting Issues

A mother is not a father. Two parents are important in rearing a child. Fathers teach children how to father. If a father is not there or unavailable, reach out to uncles, relatives, teachers, ministers, and other positive male role models, as well as mothers as mentors.

We need someone to tell fathers that they are respected. Some of us may think that men are valuable, but we need to say it out loud. We need to educate men and fathers of this fact in a variety of ways, including the following three ways.

1. **Political education:** Men need to know how the political system works.

2. **Support groups:** Young fathers and separated fathers need this support. Public health issues covered in support groups can include topics such as gang activities; the impact of drugs, alcohol, and tobacco on the mind, body, and spirit; AIDS and STDs, male victimization of women; abusive women; dietary issues; diabetes; lung cancer; hypertension; and prostate cancer.

Economic development seminars are also crucial (for example, this could include a seminar on how to make money). All fathers need something where they can get information about how to become better fathers.

3. **Community projects:** These projects bring fathers and children together, whether through games, educational activities, or social activities, the whole notion of mentoring is the aim in those small groups.

How do we get the message to the street? And how do we get the message from the street? We can do that in these ways.

- We can present a better understanding of community outreach programs and street programs and link all of these through community-based hospitals and health agencies so that the programs hit the street in the correct manner.
- We want to make it clear that our young black men are seen as a resource and not just a statistic or an opportunity for people to research. We value them at a higher level, and we need to approach them in a way that they become the messengers who try to improve the quality of life on the streets.
- We can assess the vicinity of our youths. We have no one blanket site where we can reach all our youths. We have to assess every male present for his own individual needs. No particular model would impact the entire community.
- We can give youth employment readiness and preparedness information so we can attempt to get meaningful jobs for the youths in our community. We must recognize that in preparation for a job, our kids in our communities will go up against many kids searching for jobs who have already experienced a higher income level than many of us sitting at the table in shirts and ties. We have to transcend and help them understand that, yes, they can live successfully without that big number of fast, flash cash in their pocket.

- We need positive recreational activities for our youths.
- We need to make mentoring opportunities of various levels available to students, such as from mentoring professionals and other community members.
- We need to educate men on HIV and AIDS issues; males become primary caregivers due to women dying.
- We need to make resource guides available within the community.

Everybody can be great, because everybody can serve. ...
You only need a heart full of grace. A soul generated by love.

—Dr. Martin Luther King Jr.

Therefore, we must create new vehicles and approaches to engage young men so they live healthy and productive lives. We must rise and develop new strategies to unlock the door to new opportunities. One of our greatest challenges is that we have relied on the government to save us. The statement is true in many respects. As the late President Kennedy said, "Ask not what your country can do for you; ask what can you do for your country." Incorporate yourselves with others who are willing to support your growth and development. This statement is not Democratic or Republican in nature; it is a statement of personal empowerment. We need collective engagement from the people in the community. All entities must work together as a well-oiled machine.

We as a society must break through the rubble of institutional racism, discrimination, poverty, imprisonment, and unemployment. We must elevate to a higher level and exist beyond the trails that stand before us. We must embrace our creator's greater plan for our lives. To my African American brothers and sisters and to every race under heaven, we have been created from one blood through one race, the human race. Even though many African Americans bear the pain of the past, which emotionally stains the present and possibly could dim our future, we must hold fast to Dr. King's dreams and our heavenly father's promises, hearing the voices of the patriots of old and present, saying we have come this far by faith and they will lead us to victory every step of the way.

We must hear the voices of Old Man Mathis—from the backwoods of Georgia, singing "I've got to move to a better place"—and the Woods family, Roosevelt and Jennie Alston, Johnny and Mother Mingo, Malcolm X, Martin Luther King Jr., Reverend Arturo Skinner, Reverend George Ryder, my beloved brother who I miss dearly, Uncle Frank Woods and family, Emma B. Dixon and family, Dion Bailey, Bishop and Pastor Saundra Barnes, Betty Scovil and family, and the Marrant family. We must embrace the former the president of the United States of America Barack Obama for his legacy in the black community and world, the Waller family, the Ruranga family, the Holt family, Morris and Derek, Daniel Luke, Linda and Mickel Hicks and family, Bishop Marcus Barnes and family, the Benders Oliver family, the Jackson family, the Evans family, Walter Howard, and the Charles family. For other families too, name by name, we will hold true to our testimony for generations to come that we too will rise moving forward—not holding on to the pain of yesterday but reaching forth to the greater promises of the future for our children, our grandchildren, and every family member and to the faith and the promises that we too stand in our faith in God.

In addition, thank you to all my family members for their support and love, especially my twin brother, Carl, for his technical support, along with my brothers Bobby, Edward, and Jerry; my sisters; and my uncle Frank for his generational insights and dedication. And thank you to those I interviewed, Dad and Mother Mingo, Mother Jennie and Roosevelt Austin and everyone who has contributed to my life. Today and always, I salute you with love.

Finally, Groups will convene/unit to discuss their strategies and approaches to resolve these issues.

From left: Al-Tariq Dunson, Tillard Gallop, Ed Waller, Shariff James

Mr. Charles Dixon, Mr. Anthony Williams, Mr. Al Dunson, and a Young Father in the Young Fathers Program

Rev. George Ryder speaking at the NJ Medical
School Young Fathers Program

Mr. Stacey Williams poetry recitation at a Conference
at the Deliverance Temple, Newark, New Jersey

Ms. Bernita Waller former Administrator of the Division of Adolescent & Young Adult Medicine, Newark, NJ.

Charles Dixon (far right), Dr. Linda Jones Hick (front center) and the Family Partnership Network at NJMS, recipients of community service award for serving young men and families both locally and nationally.

ENDNOTES

1. University of Illinois at Urbana-Champaign Department of English, "About the Great Depression," www.english.illinois.edu/maps/depression/about.htm.

2. "John L. Lewis," *Wikipedia*, last modified March 30, 2017, https://en.wikipedia.org/wiki/John_L._Lewis.

3. "A. Philip Randolph," *Wikipedia*, last modified April 4, 2017, https://en.wikipedia.org/wiki/A._Philip_Randolph.

4. "Great Migration (African American)," *Wikipedia*, last modified April 10, 2017, https://en.wikipedia.org/wiki/Great_Migration_(African_American).

5. Nebraska Studies, "Racial Tensions in Omaha: African American Migration," www.nebraskastudies.org/0700/frameset_reset.html?http://www.nebraskastudies.org/0700/stories/0701_0131.html.

6. "Great Migration (African American)," *Wikipedia*, last modified April 10, 2017, https://en.wikipedia.org/wiki/Great_Migration_(African_American).

7. William L. O'Neill, *A Democracy at War: America's Fight at Home and Abroad in World War II* (Cambridge, MA: Harvard University Press, 1993), 236.

8. William L. O'Neill, *A Democracy at War: America's Fight at Home and Abroad in World War II* (Cambridge, MA: Harvard University Press, 1993), 237.

9   William L. O'Neill, *A Democracy at War: America's Fight at Home and Abroad in World War II* (Cambridge, MA: Harvard University Press, 1993), 237.

10 William L. O'Neill, *A Democracy at War: America's Fight at Home and Abroad in World War II* (Cambridge, MA: Harvard University Press, 1993), 237.

11 William L. O'Neill, *A Democracy at War: America's Fight at Home and Abroad in World War II* (Cambridge, MA: Harvard University Press, 1993), 237.

12 "Tuskegee Airmen," *Wikipedia*, last modified April 6, 2017, https://en.wikipedia.org/wiki/Tuskegee_Airmen.

13 Jim Thompson, *"The Tuskegee Airman,"* last modified March 12, 2004, www.allstar.fiu.edu/aero/tuskegee.htm.

14 Jawn A. Sandifer (Ed.), *The Afro-American in United States History* (New York: Globe Book Company, 1969), 285.

15 Jawn A. Sandifer (Ed.), *The Afro-American in United States History* (New York: Globe Book Company, 1969).

16 Mary R. Sawyer, "The Black Church and Black Politics: Models of Ministerial Activism," Journal of Religious Thought, 52–53, no. 1–2 (Winter 1995–Spring 1996): 18, 45.

17 *Afro-American History Free Negros.*

18 "Madison Square Garden Crusade," *Deliverance Voice Magazine 6, no. 5* (September–October 1972).

19 Douglas J. Besharov and Peter Germanis, *"Welfare Reform: Four Years Later,"* Public Interest (Summer 2000), www.welfareacademy.org/pubs/welfare/four_yea.shtml.

20 Nancy Solomon, *"40 Years On, Newark Re-Examines Painful Riot Past,"* NPR, last modified July 14, 2017, www.npr.org/templates/story/story.php?storyId=11966375.

21. "History of the Hippie Movement," *Wikipedia*, last modified April 7, 2017, https://en.wikipedia.org/wiki/History_of_the_hippie_movement.

22. Gary Roush, *"Statistics about the Vietnam War,"* last modified June 2, 2008, www.vhfcn.org/stat.html.

23. Jawanza Kunjunfu, *Black Economics: Solutions for Economic and Community Empowerment* (African American Images, 1991), 1.

24. Susan Brownmiller, *Against Our Will: Men, Women and Rape* (New York: Fawcett, 1975).

25. Paige Z., *"Women's Movements of the 1920s and the 1960s"* (Chappaqua, NY: Horace Greeley HS), www.pptpalooza.net/PPTs/AHAP/AHAPStudent Projects/WomensMovement1920sAnd1960s-PaigeZ.ppt.

26. Howard Rosenberg, *"Examining 'The Vanishing Family,'"* Los Angeles Times, January 22, 1986, http://articles.latimes.com/1986-01-22/entertainment/ca-31681_1_vanishing-family.

27. Gil Rugh, *"Promise Keepers and the Rising Tide of Ecumenism,"* www.cnview.com/on_line_resources/promise_keepers_and_the_rising_tide_of_ecumenism.htm.

28. "Promise Keepers," *Billboard*, www.billboard.com/artist/352520/promise-keepers/biography.

29. "Interview with Four African American Men," *Home News Tribune*, October 18, 1995.

30. *Star-Ledger*, June 14, 1995.

31. Claire Gordon, "Prisons Commit Greater Crimes Than Inmates," *Yale Daily News*, March 31, 2008, http://yaledailynews.com/blog/2008/03/31/prisons-commit-greater-crimes-than-inmates.

32. Reese Erlich, "Prison Labor: Workin' for the Man," *Covert Action Quarterly* 54 (Fall 1995), http://prop1.org/legal/prisons/labor.htm.

33. Nicholas Confessore, "Prisoner Proliferation," *The American Prospect* (September–October 1999), http://prospect.org/article/prisoner-proliferation.

34 "American's Prisoners a Corporate Workforce," *The American Prospect* (September–October 1999): 66.

35 Reese Erlich, "Prison Labor: Workin' for the Man," *Covert Action Quarterly* 54 (Fall 1995), http://prop1.org/legal/prisons/labor.htm.

36 Reese Erlich, "Prison Labor: Workin' for the Man," *Covert Action Quarterly* 54 (Fall 1995), http://prop1.org/legal/prisons/labor.htm.

37 Reese Erlich, "Prison Labor: Workin' for the Man," *Covert Action Quarterly* 54 (Fall 1995), http://prop1.org/legal/prisons/labor.htm.

38 Reese Erlich, "Prison Labor: Workin' for the Man," *Covert Action Quarterly* 54 (Fall 1995), http://prop1.org/legal/prisons/labor.htm.

39 Phil Smith, "Private Prisons: Profits of Crime, More Money," *Covert Action Quarterly* 2 (Fall 1993).

40 John E. Widenman, "Doing Time, Marking Race," *The Nation* 261, no. 14 (1995): 503–506.

41 Joseph F. Sullivan, "Whitman Apologizes for Remark on Blacks," *New York Times*, April 14, 1995, www.nytimes.com/1995/04/14/nyregion/whitman-apologizes-for-remark-on-blacks.html.

42 From an audio recording by a Newark, New Jersey, resident.

www.ingramcontent.com/pod-product-compliance
Lightning Source LLC
Chambersburg PA
CBHW021447070526
44577CB00002B/293